Crochet For Belly Dancers

Crochet for Belly Dancers

By Stacy Vaka

Crochet Kitten

Manassas, Virginia

ISBN 978-1-7369551-4-7

Scripture taken from the New King James Version®. Copyright © 1982 by Thomas Nelson. Used by permission. All rights reserved.

Crochet stitch symbols by StitchinCrochet Pro™.

Printed in the United States of America.

Published by Crochet Kitten: PO Box 4289, Manassas, VA 20108

Every effort has been made to ensure that the instructions in this book are complete and accurate. However, responsibility cannot be taken for human error, typographical mistakes, or variations in individual work. Please contact curiosity@crochetkitten.com if pattern support is needed.

www.CrochetKitten.com

This book is for my sisters in dance who stand with me at that intersection between wholesome and exotic.

...You shall again be adorned with your tambourines,
And shall go forth in the dances of those who rejoice.

— Jeremiah 31:4

Table of Contents

Introduction

My greatest joy as a dancer comes from the opportunity to create art—not just the physical kind that transforms emotions and music into a visual display, but also the constructive kind that results in a unique costume that describes who I am as a dancer.

I learned how to crochet 8 years before I ventured into the world of belly dancing, so it was only natural that as soon as I needed a belly dance costume, I began to consider how I might crochet one for myself. These are my original designs, some from my days as a baby belly dancer, and some inspired and commissioned by my first belly dance troupe, the Suburban Gypsies. The collection is particularly special to me because they show my evolution both as a designer and as a belly dancer.

I hope they help you to find your own uniqueness as a dancer, both in choreography and in costume.

Stacy Vaka

Dance Shrug

This shrug is incredibly simple to make, despite being made from a thinner yarn, and it will keep you warm during chilly winter dance practices. If you find the mohair difficult to work with, you may choose to work with the silk by itself.

Pattern Level

Basic / De base / Básico

Finished Sizes

Women's XS (**S**, M, **L**, 1X, **2X**, 3X, **4X**, 5X)

Girls' 2T (**4T**, 6, **8**, 10, **12**, 14, **16**)

Materials

SUPER FINE

Women's Shrug

- 2 (**2**, 2, **2**, 2, **3**, 3, **3**, 3) skeins Cascade Heritage Silk
- 2 (**2**, 2, **3**, 3, **3**, 4, **4**, 4) balls Cascade Kid Seta
- Size H-8 (5.0mm) crochet hook or size to obtain gauge

Girls' Shrug

- 1 (**1**, 1, **1**, 1, **1**, 1, **2**) skeins Cascade Heritage Silk
- 1 (**1**, 1, **2**, 2, **2**, 2, **2**) balls Cascade Kid Seta
- Size H-8 (5.0mm) crochet hook or size to obtain gauge

Gauge Square

Row 1. Ch 23. Dc in 4th ch from hook and ea rem ch across (20 dc).

Rows 2-9. Ch 3; turn. Dc in flo ea dc across. Finish off.

20 dc and 9 rows = 4 inches

Note

Pattern is written for smallest size with changes for larger sizes in parentheses. To avoid confusion, it may be helpful to circle the numbers corresponding to your size before beginning this project. When only one number is given, it applies to all sizes.

Women's Shrug

Worked sideways from cuff to cuff.

With both yarns held together, ch 28 (**32**, 37, **41**, 41, **41**, 48, **49**, 54).

Rnd 1. Dc in fourth ch from hook and ea rem ch across. Join with sl st in top of beg ch. *25 (29, 34, 38, 38, 38, 45, 46, 51) dc.*

Rnd 2. Ch 3; turn. 2 dc in flo of first dc, dc in flo of ea rem dc around. Join with sl st in t ch. *26 (30, 35, 39, 39, 39, 46, 47, 52) dc.*

Rnds 3-21 (3-17, 3-17, 3-17, 3-24, 3-33, 3-33, 3-38, 3-38). Rep rnd 2. *45 (45, 50, 54, 61, 70, 77, 83, 88) dc.*

Rnds 22-41 (18-42, 18-43, 18-44, 25-45, 34-46, 34-47, 39-48, 39-49). Ch 3; turn. Dc in flo of ea dc around. Join with sl st in t-ch.

The next section is worked in rows without joining.

Rows 42-84 (43-87, 44-92, **45-97,** 46-98, **47-102,** 48-103, **49-107,** 40-109**).** Ch 3; turn. Dc in flo of ea dc across. *Do not join between rows.*

The next section is worked in rnds again.

Rnds 85-104 (88-112, 93-117, **98-124,** 99-119, **103-115,** 104-117, **108-117,** 110-120**).** Ch 3; turn. Dc in flo of ea dc around. Join with sl st in t-ch.

Rnds 105-124 (113-128, 118-133, **125-140,** 120-142, **116-147,** 118-149, **118-154,** 121-157**).** Ch 3; turn. Dc2tog in flo of first 2 dc; dc in flo of ea rem dc around. Join with sl st in t-ch. *25 (29, 34, 38, 38, 38, 45, 46, 51) dc.*

Rnd 125 (129, 134, **141,** 143, **148,** 150, **155,** 158**).** Ch 3; turn. Dc in flo of ea dc around. Join with sl st in t-ch. Finish off.

Edging
With both yarns held together, join yarn with sl st in center of back. Ch 1; sc evenly around chest opening. Join with sl st in first sc. Finish off.

Girls' Shrug
Worked sideways from cuff to cuff.

With both yarns held together, ch 22 (**23,** 26, **26,** 28, **28,** 28, **28**).

Rnd 1. Dc in fourth ch from hook and ea rem ch across. Join with sl st in top of beg ch. *19 (20, 23, 23, 25, 25, 25, 25) dc.*

Rnd 2. Ch 3; turn. 2 dc in flo of first dc, dc in flo of ea rem dc around. Join with sl st in t-ch. *20 (21, 24, 24, 26, 26, 26, 26) dc.*

Rnds 3-14 (3-15, 3-14, **3-16,** 3-15, **3-17,** 3-18, **3-19).** Rep rnd 2. *32 (34, 36, 38, 39, 41, 42, 43) dc.*

Rnds 15-22 (16-26, 15-29, **17-31,** 16-34, **18-38,** 19-40, **20-42).** Ch 3; turn. Dc in flo of ea dc around. Join with sl st in t-ch.

The next section is worked in rows without joining.

Rows 23-50 (27-56, 30-60, **32-65,** 35-69, **39-76,** 41-80, **43-84).** Ch 3; turn. Dc in flo of ea dc across. *Do not join between rows.*

The next section is worked in rnds again.

Rnds 51-57 (57-66, 61-74, **66-79,** 70-87, **77-96,** 81-101, **85-106).** Ch 3; turn. Dc in flo of ea dc around. Join with sl st in t-ch.

Rnds 58-70 (67-80, 75-87, **80-94,** 88-101, **97-112,** 102-118, **107-124).** Ch 3; turn. Dc2tog in flo of first 2 dc; dc in flo of ea rem dc around. Join with sl st in t-ch. *19 (20, 23, 23, 25, 25, 25, 25) dc.*

Rnd 71 (81, 88, **95,** 102, **113,** 119, **125).** Ch 3; turn. Dc in flo of ea dc around. Join with sl st in t-ch. Finish off.

Edging
With both yarns held together, join yarn with sl st in center of back. Ch 1; sc evenly around chest opening. Join with sl st in first sc. Finish off.

Cassie Leg Warmers

These leg warmers are great for growing girls because the ribbon laces make them even more adjustable. If you find the mohair difficult to work with, you may omit it and work with the silk alone.

Pattern Level

Easy / Facile / Fácil

Finished Sizes
2-5 years (**5-9 years**, 7-13 years, **Adult Small**, Adult Medium, **Adult Large**)

Materials

SUPER FINE

- 1 skein Cascade Heritage Silk
- 1 ball Cascade Kid Seta
- Size H-8 (5.0mm) crochet hook or size to obtain gauge
- *Optional:* 1.5 (**1.75**, 2, **2**, 2, **2.25**) yd 3/8-inch wide ribbon

Gauge Square
Row 1. Ch 23. Dc in 4th ch from hook and ea rem ch across (20 dc).

Rows 2-9. Ch 3; turn. Dc in flo ea dc across. Finish off.

20 dc and 9 rows = 4 inches

Note
Pattern is written for smallest size with changes for larger sizes in parentheses. To avoid confusion, it may be helpful to circle the numbers corresponding to your size before beginning this project. When only one number is given, it applies to all sizes.

Leg Warmers

With both yarns held together, ch 43 (**43**, 53, **53**, 53, **63**), leaving a long tail for weaving.

Rnd 1. Dc in fourth ch from hook, dc in next 3 ch, *skip next 2 ch; eyelet made. Dc in next 4 ch, ch 2, dc in next 4 ch; rep from * across to last 6 ch. Skip next 2 ch, dc in next 3 ch, 2 dc in last ch. Join with sl st at top of beg ch. *33 (33, 41, 41, 41, 49) dc.*

Rnd 2. Ch 3; turn. Dc in flo of first 4 dc, *skip next 2 dc, dc in flo of next 3 dc, (dc, ch 2, dc) in next ch-2 sp, dc in flo of next 3 dc; rep from * across to last 5 dc. Skip next 2 dc, dc in flo of last 3 dc, 2 dc in same st as joining. Join with dc in top of t-ch.

Rnds 3-18 (3-22, 3-26, **3-26**, 3-28, **3-30).** Rep rnd 2.

Finish off.

Finishing

Use the tail left at the beginning to sew the gap closed on the beginning end of the legwarmer. Weave in all remaining ends. If ribbon is desired, cut ribbon into two equal lengths. Lace ribbon through the first and last eyelets of every other row so that they cross over the joins of each row. Tie ribbon at the top.

Dancer's Sling Bag

While a belly dancer needs nothing more than her own body to practice her craft, this bag comes in especially handy at conventions. It is roomy enough to fit a water, hip scarves, notebook, and more.

Pattern Level

Easy / Facile / Fácil

Finished Size
22" wide by 22" high.

Materials

MEDIUM

- 400 yd 5/bulky weight yarn
- Size J-10 (6.0 mm) crochet hook
- Yarn needle
- 1 yd fabric for lining
- Sewing thread in coordinating color
- Sewing needle

Motif — make 4.

Ch 18.

Row 1. Dc in 6th ch from hook (first 5 ch count as 1 dc and 1 ch-1 sp), (ch 1, skip next ch, dc in next ch) 6 times. *8 dc and 7 ch-1 sp.*

Row 2. Ch 4 (counts as 1 dc and 1 ch-1 sp); turn. Skip first dc ch-1 sp, dc in next dc, (ch 1, skip next ch-1 sp, dc in next dc) 5 times, ch 1, skip last ch-1 sp, dc in last dc.

Rows 4-6. Rep row 2.

Row 7. Rep row 2. Do not finish off.

Motif is worked in rounds without turning from this point forward.

Rnd 1. Rotate motif clockwise and work down end of rows: (sl st, ch 1, 2 sc) in next sp, 2 sc in ea of next 2 sp, (sc, ch 4, sc) in next sp, 2 sc in ea of next 2 sp, (2 sc, ch 1, 2 sc) in next sp; corner made. *Rotate motif clockwise: *2 sc in ea of next 2 sp, (sc, ch 4, sc) in next sp, 2 sc in ea of next 2 sp, (2 sc, ch 1, 2 sc) in next sp; corner made. Rep from * once. Rotate motif clockwise: 2 sc in ea of next 2 ch-1 sp, (sc, ch 4, sc) in next ch-1 sp, 2 sc in ea of next 2 ch-1 sp, 2 sc in next ch-1 sp, ch 1, join with sl st in first sc; beg corner made. *56 sc, 4 ch-4 sp, and 1 ch-1 sp.*

Rnd 2. Do not turn. Sl st in first 5 sc, skip next sc, (5 picot, sc) in next ch-4 sp, skip next sc, sl st in next 6 sc, *sc in next ch-1 sp, sl st in next 6 sc, skip next sc, (5 picot, sc) in next ch-4 sp, skip next sc, sl st in next 6 sc; rep from * twice. Sc in next ch-1 sp, join with sl st in first sl st. Finish off. *20 picot.*

Rnd 3. Join with sl st in any corner sc. Ch 1, sc in same sc as joining, ch 5, skip first picot, sc in next picot, ch 6, skip next picot, sc in next picot, ch 5, *sc in next corner sc, ch 5, skip first picot, sc in next picot, ch 6, skip next picot, sc in next picot, ch 5; rep from * twice. Join with sl st in first sc. *12 sc, 8 ch-5 sp, and 4 ch-6 sp.*

Rnd 4. Ch 1, sc in same sc as joining, 5 sc in first ch-5 sp, sc in next sc, (4 sc, ch 2, 4 sc) in next ch-6 sp, sc in next sc, 5 sc in next ch-5 sp, *sc in next sc,

5 sc in next ch-5 sp, sc in next sc, (4 sc, ch 2, 4 sc) in next ch-6 sp, sc in next sc, 5 sc in next ch-5 sp; rep from * twice. Join with sl st in first sc. *84 sc and 4 ch-2 sp.*

Rnd 5. Ch 1, sc in same sc as joining, sc in next 10 sc, (sc, ch 2, sc) in next ch-2 sp, *sc in next 21 sc, (sc, ch 2, sc) in next ch-2 sp; rep from * twice. Sc in next 10 sc, join with sl st in first sc. Finish off. *92 sc and 4 ch-2 sp.*

Rnd 6. Join yarn with sl st in any corner ch-2 sp. Ch 5 (counts as 1 dc and 1 ch-2 sp), dc in same ch-2 sp, ch 1, (skip next sc, dc in next sc, ch 1) 11 times, *(dc, ch 2, dc) in next ch-2 sp, ch 1, (skip next sc, dc in next sc, ch 1) 11 times; rep from * twice. Join with sl st in 3rd ch of beg ch-5. *52 dc, 48 ch-1 sp, and 4 ch-2 sp.*

Rnd 7. Ch 1, sc in same ch as joining, 3 sc in first ch-2 sp, *sc in ea dc and ch-1 sp across to next ch-2 sp, 3 sc in next ch-2 sp; rep from * twice. Sc in ea dc and ch-1 sp across to first ch-2 sp, join with sl st in first sc. Finish off. *112 sc.*

Back Panel

Worked in rounds without turning.

Ch 60.

Row 1. Dc in 6th ch from hook (counts as 1 dc and 1 ch-1 sp), *ch 1, skip next ch, dc in next ch; rep from * across. *29 dc and 28 ch-1 sp.*

Rows 2-28. Ch 4 (counts as 1 dc and 1 ch); turn. Skip first dc and first ch-1 sp, dc in next dc, *ch 1, skip next ch-1 sp, dc in next dc; rep from * across.

Finish off.

Assembly

Whipstitch Motifs together in a 2 x 2 pattern; Front Panel made. Sc Back Panel and Front Panel together by sc evenly around sides and bottom, leaving Top Edge open. Finish off.

Top Edge

Join yarn with sl st in any sc on Top Edge.

Rnd 1. Ch 1, work 112 sc evenly around Top Edge. Join with sl st in first sc. *112 sc.*

Rnd 2. Ch 4, skip first 2 sc, dc in next sc, *ch 1, skip next sc, dc in next sc; rep from * around to last sc. Ch 1, skip last sc, join with sl st in 3rd ch of beg ch-4.

Rnd 3. Ch 1, sc in same ch as joining, sc in ea ch-1 sp and dc around. *112 sc.*

Rnd 4. Ch 1, sc in same ch as joining, sc in ea sc around. Finish off. Weave in all ends.

Lining

Fold fabric to be used for lining in half so it is double-thick. Lie bag flat on fabric and, using bag as template, cut fabric around bag, leaving a ¼-inch seam allowance. You will now have two fabric panels of equal size. Sew the two fabric panels together along sides and bottom, leaving top open. Pin lining into bag and sew into place along top.

Strap

*Join with sl st in first bottom corner. Ch 168. Remove hook and weave ch in and out of ch-1 sp of rnd 2 of Top Edge. Replace hook and join with sl st in second bottom corner. Finish off. Rep from * to double the strap. Weave in all ends.

Gypsy Rose Halter

The beauty of this design is in its simplicity. A single motif adorns an entire dancer, making it incredibly easy to outfit an entire troupe.

Pattern Level

Easy / Facile / Fácil

Finished Sizes

S/M (**L/1X**, 2X/3X, **4X/5X**)

Materials

BULKY

- 1 (**2**, 3, **5**) skeins Cascade Rabat
- Size J-10 (6.0mm) crochet hook

Gauge Square

Rnd 1. Ch 4; join with sl st in first ch to make a ring. Ch 3 (counts as 1 dc), 2 dc in ring, ch 3, (3 dc, ch 3) in ring 3 times; join with sl st in top of beg ch. Finish off.

Rnd 2. Join yarn with sl st in any ch-3 sp. Ch 3 (counts as dc), (2 dc, ch 3, 3 dc) in same ch-sp, ch 1, *(3 dc, ch 3, 3 dc) in next ch-sp, ch 1; rep from * around. Join with sl st in top of beg ch. Finish off.

Rnd 3. Join yarn with sl st in any ch-3 sp. Ch 3 (counts as dc, (2 dc, ch 3, 3 dc) in same ch-sp, ch 1, *3 dc in next ch-1 sp, ch 1, (3 dc, ch 3, 3 dc) in next ch-3 sp, ch 1; rep from * around. Finish off.

3 rnds = 6 inches measured diagonally from corner to corner.

Special Stitches

3-tr cluster. *YO twice, insert hook in indicated st, pull up a loop, (YO and draw through 2 loops) twice; rep from * 2 more times. YO and draw through all 4 loops on hook. 3-tr cluster complete.

3-dtr cluster. *YO 3 times, insert hook in indicated st, pull up a loop, (YO and draw through 2 loops) 3 times, rep from * 2 more times. YO and draw through all 4 loops on hook. 3-dtr cluster complete.

Note

Pattern is written for smallest size with changes for larger sizes in parentheses. To avoid confusion, it may be helpful to circle the numbers corresponding to your size before beginning this project. When only one number is given, it applies to all sizes.

Directions

Ch 6. Join with sl st to form a ring.

Rnd 1. Ch 5 (counts as 1 dc and 2 ch), (dc in ring, ch 2) 7 times. Join with sl st in third ch of beg ch. *8 dc and 8 ch-2 sp.*

Rnd 2. (Sc, hdc, 3 dc, hdc, sc) in ea ch-sp around. Join with sl st in first sc. *8 petals.*

Rnd 3. Keeping the ch *behind* the petals of the previous rnd, *ch 4, sc between next 2 petals; rep from * around. *8 ch-4 sp.*

Rnd 4. (Sc, hdc, 5 dc, hdc, sc) in ea ch-sp around. Join with sl st in first sc. *8 petals.*

Rnd 5. Rep rnd 3.

Rnd 6. (Sc, hdc, 7 dc, hdc, sc) in ea ch-sp around. Join with sl st in first sc. *8 petals.*

Rnd 7. Rep rnd 3.

Rnd 8. (Sc, hdc, dc, 7 tr, dc, hdc, sc) in ea ch-sp around. Join with sl st in first sc. *8 petals.*

Rnd 9. Sl st in ea st up to center tr of next petal. Sc in same tr, *ch 7, (3-tr cluster, ch 4, 3-dtr cluster, ch 4, 3-tr cluster) in center tr of next petal, ch 7, sc in center tr of next petal; rep from * around, ending with a sl st in first sc of rnd. *8 ch-7 sp.*

Rnd 10. Sl st in next ch-7 sp, ch 3 (counts as dc), (2 dc, ch 1, 3 dc) in same ch-7 sp, ch 1, 3 dc in next ch-4 sp, ch 1, (3 dc, ch 3, 3 dc) in 3-dtr cluster, ch 1, 3 dc in next ch-4 sp, ch 1, *(3 dc, ch 1, 3 dc, ch 1) in ea of next 2 ch-7 sp, 3 dc in next ch-4 sp, ch 1, (3 dc, ch 3, 3 dc) in 3-dtr cluster, ch 1, 3 dc in next ch-4 sp, ch 1; rep from * twice more. (3 dc, ch 1, 3 dc) in next ch-7 sp, ch 1; join with sl st in top of beg ch.

Sizes L/1X, 2X/3X, and 4X/5X only
Rnd 11. Ch 3, 2 dc in last ch-1 sp (to the *right* of the beg ch-3), *(ch 1, 3 dc) in ea ch-1 sp across to next ch-3 sp, (ch 1, 3 dc, ch 3, 3 dc) in next ch-3 sp; rep from * around to last ch-3 sp. (Ch 1, 3 dc) in ea rem ch-1 sp around to beg ch. Ch 1, join with sl st in top of beg ch.

Sizes 2X/3X and 4X/5X only
Rnd 12. Rep rnd 11.

Size 4X/5X only
Rnd 13. Rep rnd 11.

All Sizes
Last Rnd. Ch 1. Sc in ea dc and ch-sp around, working 3 sc in ea corner. Join with sl st in first sc. Finish off.

Neck Ties

Join yarn with sl st in any corner. Ch 40 (**45**, **50**, **55**). Finish off. Rep in same corner for a total of 2 ties at the neck.

Mid-Back Ties

Join yarn with sl st in corner to the right of the Neck Ties. Ch 40 (**45**, **50**, **55**). Finish off. Rep in corner to the left of Neck Ties for a total of 2 mid-back ties.

Fringe

Cut 34 (**38**, **42**, **46**) 6-inch pieces of yarn. Tie 2 pieces in each of the ch-1 sp between the mid-back ties. Trim evenly.

Mother–Daughter Silk Shrug and Coin Belt

This design was inspired by the luxurious, yet ecological yarns spun in India from recycled silk saris. These yarns are quite bulky, but bulky yarns make for quick projects, which means an ideal pattern for troupe costuming. The open stitch pattern gives wearable drape to the final project.

Pattern Level

Easy / Facile / Fácil

Finished Sizes

Women's XS (**S**, M, **L**, 1X, **2X**, 3X, **4X**, 5X)

Girls' 2T (**4T**, 6, **8**, 10, **12**, 14, **16**)

Materials

SUPER BULKY

Mother's Set

- 6 (**6**, 6, **7**, 8, **10**, 10, **11**, 12) skeins Recycled Silk Sari Yarn
- 1 ball Aunt Lydia's Crochet Thread Metallic, Size 10
- Size N-15 (10.0mm) crochet hook
- 34 (**37**, 40, **43**, 45, **49**, 50, **52**, 55) Chinese coins

Daughter's Set

- 2 (**3**, 3, **4**, 4, **4**, 5, **5**) skeins Recycled Silk Sari Yarn
- 1 ball Aunt Lydia's Crochet Thread Metallic, Size 10

- Size N-15 (10.0mm) crochet hook
- *Optional:* 22 (**25**, 25, **28**, 30, **31**, 33, **36**) Chinese coins

Gauge Square

Row 1. Ch 13. Dc in 5th ch from hook, *ch 1, skip 1 ch, dc in next ch; rep from * across.

Row 2. Ch 4; turn. Skip first dc, *dc in next ch sp, ch 1; rep from * across, ending with 1 dc in t-ch.

Rows 3-4. Rep row 2.

Finish off. 4 reps and 4 rows = 4 inches

Pattern Notes

Pattern is written for smallest size with changes for larger sizes in parentheses. To avoid confusion, it may be helpful to circle the numbers corresponding to your size before beginning this project. When only one number is given, it applies to all sizes.

Mother's Shrug — make 2 panels.

Worked from top down. One panel is the front of the choli; the other is the back. Both panels are worked the same.

With sari yarn and N hook, ch 105 (**111**, 111, **117**, 117, **123**, 123, **123**, 123).

Row 1. Dc in 5th ch from hook, *ch 1, skip 1 ch, dc in next ch; rep from * across. *52 (55, 55, 58, 58, 61, 61, 61, 61) dc.*

Row 2. Ch 4; turn. Skip first dc, *dc in next ch sp, ch 1; rep from * across, ending with 1 dc in t-ch.

Rows 3-5 (3-5, 3-5, 3-6, 3-6, 3-7, 3-8, 3-9 3-9).
Rep row 2.

Finish off.

Assembly
Lay front panel on top of back panel. With sari yarn, whipstitch along top edge from cuff to the 19th (**20th**, 20th, **20th**, 20th, **21st**, 21st, **21st**, 21st) dc in from the edge on both sides to create the top seam of the sleeves. Repeat for the bottom seam of the sleeves.

Neck Edging
With sari yarn and N hook, join yarn with sl st in any dc in the neckline. Ch 1; sc in same dc as joining and in ea ch sp and dc around. Join with sl st in first dc. Finish off.

Bottom Edging
String 16 (**17**, 17, **19**, 19, **20**, 20, **20**, 20) coins onto sari yarn. With N hook, join yarn with sl st in any dc in bottom edge.

Row 1. Ch 1, sc in same dc, ch 5, *skip next dc, sc in next dc, ch 5; rep from * around. Join with sl st in first sc. *16 (17, 17, 19, 19, 20, 20, 20, 20) ch sp.*

Row 2. Ch 1; turn. *(3 sc, ch 1, slide 1 coin up to hook, ch 2, 3 sc) in next ch sp; rep from * around. Join with sl st in first sc. Finish off.

Mother's Coin Belt

Worked in the round from the top down.

With sari yarn and N hook, ch 75 (**81**, 93, **99**, 105, **117**, 123, **129**, 141).

Row 1. Dc in 5th ch from hook, *ch 1, skip 1 ch, dc in next ch; rep from * across. Join with sl st in

first dc to form a ring. *37 (40, 46, 49, 52, 58, 61, 64, 70) dc.*

Row 2. Ch 4; turn. Skip first dc, *dc in next ch sp, ch 1; rep from * across. Sl st in t-ch.

Rows 3-5. Rep row 2.

Finish off.

Top Edging
With sari yarn and N hook, join yarn with sl st in first ch of top edge. Ch 1; sc in same ch as joining and in ea ch across. Do not join with sl st in first sc; the small gap at the top will help for getting in and out of the coin belt. Finish off.

Bottom Edging
String 18 (**20**, 23, **24**, 26, **29**, 30, **32**, 35) coins onto sari yarn. With N hook, join yarn with sl st in any dc in bottom edge.

Row 1. Ch 1, sc in same dc, ch 5, *skip next dc, sc in next dc, ch 5; rep from * around. Join with sl st in first sc. *18 (20, 23, 24, 26, 29, 30, 32, 35) ch sp.*

Row 2. Ch 1; turn. *(3 sc, ch 1, slide 1 coin up to hook, ch 2, 3 sc) in next ch sp; rep from * around. Join with sl st in first sc. Finish off.

Tie
With thread and F hook, ch 200 (**210**, 230, **250**, 265, **290**, 300, **305**, 330). Finish off. Knot both ends and trim excess.

Daughter's Shrug — make 2 panels.

Worked from top down. One panel is the front of the choli; the other is the back. Both panels are worked the same.

With sari yarn and N hook, ch 63 (**69**, 75, **81**, 87, **93**, 99, **105**).

Row 1. Dc in 5th ch from hook, *ch 1, skip 1 ch, dc in next ch; rep from * across. *31 (**34**, 37, **40**, 43, **46**, 49, **52**) dc.*

Row 2. Ch 4; turn. Skip first dc, *dc in next ch sp, ch 1; rep from * across, ending with 1 dc in t-ch.

Rows 3 (3-4, 3-4, 3-4, 3-4, 3-4, 3-4, 3-5). Rep row 2.

Finish off.

Assembly
Lay front panel on top of back panel. With sari yarn, whipstitch along top edge from cuff to the 10th (**12th**, 14th, **15th**, 16th, **17th**, 18th, **19th**) dc in from the edge on both sides to create the top seam of the sleeves. Repeat for the bottom seam of the sleeves.

Neck Edging
With sari yarn and N hook, join yarn with sl st in any dc in the neckline. Ch 1; sc in same dc as joining and in ea ch sp and dc around. Join with sl st in first dc. Finish off.

Bottom Edging
If adding coins, string 10 (**11**, 11, **13**, 13, **14**, 15, **16**) coins onto sari yarn. With N hook, join yarn with sl st in any dc in bottom edge.

Row 1. Ch 1, sc in same dc, ch 5, *skip next dc, sc in next dc, ch 5; rep from * around. Join with sl st in first sc. *10 (**11**, 11, **13**, 13, **14**, 15, **16**) ch sp.*

Row 2 (if using coins). Ch 1; turn. *(3 sc, ch 1, slide 1 coin up to hook, ch 2, 3 sc) in next ch sp;

rep from * around. Join with sl st in first sc. Finish off.

Row 2 (if omitting coins). Ch 1; turn. *(4 sc, ch 3, sl st in last sc made to form picot, 3 sc) in next ch sp; rep from * around. Join with sl st in first sc. Finish off.

Daughter's Coin Belt

Worked in the round from the top down.

With sari yarn and N hook, ch 51 (**57**, 57, **63**, 69, **69**, 75, **81**).

Row 1. Dc in 5th ch from hook, *ch 1, skip 1 ch, dc in next ch; rep from * across. Join with sl st in first dc to form a ring. *25 (**28**, 28, **31**, 34, **34**, 37, **40**) dc.*

Row 2. Ch 4; turn. Skip first dc, *dc in next ch sp, ch 1; rep from * across. Sl st in t-ch.

Rows 3-4. Rep row 2.

Finish off.

Top Edging
With sari yarn and N hook, join yarn with sl st in first ch of top edge. Ch 1; sc in same ch as joining and in ea ch across. *Do not join with sl st in first sc;* the small gap at the top will help for getting in and out of the coin belt. Finish off.

Bottom Edging
If adding coins, string 12 (**14**, 14, **15**, 17, **17**, 18, **20**) coins onto sari yarn. With N hook, join yarn with sl st in any dc in bottom edge.

Row 1. Ch 1, sc in same dc, ch 5, *skip next dc, sc in next dc, ch 5; rep from * around. Join with sl st in first sc. *12 (14, 14, 15, 17, 17, 18, 20) ch sp.*

Row 2 (if using coins). Ch 1; turn. *(3 sc, ch 1, slide 1 coin up to hook, ch 2, 3 sc) in next ch sp; rep from * around. Join with sl st in first sc. Finish off.

Row 2 (if omitting coins). Ch 1; turn. *(4 sc, ch 3, sl st in last sc made to form picot, 3 sc) in next ch

.

sp; rep from * around. Join with sl st in first sc. Finish off.

Tie
With thread and F hook, ch 150 (**155**, 160, **175**, 180, **190**, 200, **210**). Finish off. Knot both ends and trim excess.

Josephine Tribal Set

Pattern Level

Intermediate / Intermédiaire / Intermedio

Finished Sizes
XS (**S**, M, **L**, 1X, **2X**, 3X, **4X**, 5X)

Materials

- Main Color: Cascade Luna, 6 (**7**, 8, **9**, 11, **13**, 14, **15**, 17) hanks
- Tassels: Cascade Luna Paints, 2 hanks
- Beads, 5/8-inch length: 37 (**41**, 43, **47**, 49, **55**, 59, **60**, 66)
- Size H-8 (5.0mm) crochet hook or size to obtain gauge
- Hairpin lace loom
- Yarn needle

Gauge Square
Row 1. Ch 18. Dc in 3rd ch from hook (first 3 ch count as dc) and ea rem ch across.

Rows 2-8. Ch 3; turn. Dc in ea dc across.

16 dc and 8 rows = 4 inches.

Note
Pattern is written for smallest size with changes for larger sizes in parentheses. To avoid confusion, it may be helpful to circle the numbers corresponding to your size before beginning this project. When only one number is given, it applies to all sizes.

Right Cup - worked from bottom up.
Ch 50 (**54**, 58, **66**, 70, **74**, 82, **90**, 94).

Row 1 (RS). Dc in 4th ch from hook (counts as dc) and next 22 (**24**, 26, **30**, 32, **34**, 38, **42**, 44) ch. Leave rem ch un-worked. *24 (26, 28, 32, 34, 36, 40, 44, 46) dc.*

Row 2 (WS). Ch 3; turn. Dc in next 10 (**11**, 12, **14**, 15, **16**, 18, **20**, 21) dc, 2 dc in next 2 dc, dc in ea rem dc across. *26 (28, 30, 34, 36, 38, 42, 46, 48) dc.*

Row 3. Ch 3; turn. Dc in ea dc across.

Sizes M - 5X only
Row 4. Ch 3; turn. Dc in next - (-, 13, **15**, 16, **17**, 19, **21**, 22) dc, 2 dc in next 2 dc, dc in ea rem dc across. *- (-, 32, 36, 38, 40, 44, 48, 50) dc.*

Row 5. Ch 3; turn. Dc in ea dc across.

Sizes 1X - 5X only
Row 6. Ch 3; turn. Dc in next - (-, -, -, 17, **18**, 20, **22**, 23) dc, 2 dc in next 2 dc, dc in ea rem dc across. *- (-, -, -, 40, 42, 46, 50, 52) dc.*

Row 7. Ch 3; turn. Dc in ea dc across.

Sizes 3X - 5X only
Row 8. Ch 3; turn. Dc in next - (-, -, -, -, -, 21, **23**, 24) dc, 2 dc in next 2 dc, dc in ea rem dc across. *- (-, -, -, -, -, 48, 52, 54) dc.*

All Sizes

Rows 4 (4, 6-8, **6-8,** 8-12, **8-12,** 9-16, **9-16,** 9-16**).** Ch 3; turn. Dc in ea dc across. *26 (28, 32, 36, 40, 42, 48, 52, 54) dc.*

Row 5 (5, 9, **9,** 13, **13,** 17, **17,** 17**).** Ch 3; turn. Dc2tog over next 2 dc, dc in next 7 (8, 7, **9,** 8, **9,** 9, **11,** 12) dc, (dc2tog over next 2 dc, dc in next dc) 2 (2, 4, 4, 6, **6,** 8, 8, 8) times, dc in ea rem dc across to last 3 dc, dc2tog over next 2 dc, dc in last dc. *22 (24, 26, 30, 32, 34, 38, 42, 44) dc.*

Row 6 (6, 10, **10,** 14, **14,** 18, **18,** 18**).** Ch 3; turn. Dc2tog over next 2 dc, dc in ea rem dc across to last 3 dc, dc2tog over next 2 dc, dc in last dc. *20 (22, 24, 28, 30, 32, 36, 40, 42) dc.*

Rows 7-14 (7-15, 11-20, **11-22,** 15-27, **15-28,** 19-34, **19-36,** 19-37**).** Rep previous row. *4 dc.*

Row 15 (16, 21, **23,** 28, **29,** 35, **37,** 38**).** Ch 3; turn. Dc2tog over next 2 dc, dc in last dc. *3 dc.*

Rows 16-28 (17-30, 22-36, **24-40,** 29-47, **30-49,** 36-56, **38-58,** 39-59**).** Ch 3; turn. Dc in ea dc across.

Finish off.

Left Cup - worked from bottom up.
Left Cup is worked in un-worked ch of beg ch from Right Cup. With RS facing, join yarn with sl st in first un-worked ch. Ch 3 (counts as dc); do not turn.

Row 1. Dc in ea rem un-worked ch across. *24 (26, 28, 32, 34, 36, 40, 44, 46) dc.*

Rows 2-28 (2-30, 2-36, **2-40,** 2-47, **2-49,** 2-56, **2-58,** 2-59**).** Work the same as for Right Cup.

Finish off.

Tassel Belt - worked from top down.
Tassel Belt is worked along bottom edge of Right and Left Cups in unused loops of beg ch. With RS facing, join yarn with sl st in first unused loop of beg ch. Ch 6; do not turn.

Row 1. Skip first 3 ch, sc in next ch, *ch 6, skip next 3 ch, sc in next ch; rep from * across. *12 (13, 14, 16, 17, 18, 20, 22, 23) ch-6 sp.*

Row 2. Ch 4; turn. Sc in first ch-6 sp, *ch 3, sc in next ch-6 sp; rep from * across. Ch 1, dc in bottom of t-ch of previous row. *11 (12, 13, 15, 16, 17, 19, 21, 22) ch-3 sp.*

Row 3. Ch 4; turn. *3 dc in next sc, ch 1; rep from * across. Dc in 3rd ch of t-ch. *37 (40, 43, 49, 52, 55, 61, 67, 70) dc.*

Row 4. Ch 1; turn. *Sc in next ch-sp, ch 6; rep from * across. Sc in 3rd ch of t-ch. Finish off. *12 (13, 14, 16, 17, 18, 20, 22, 23) ch-6 sp.*

Side Ties

Left Side Tie

With RS facing, join yarn with sl st in bottom of Row 1 of Left Cup. Ch 1; do not turn.

Row 1. Work 16 sc evenly up first 8 rows of Left Cup. Leave rem outer edge un-worked. *16 sc.*

Row 2. Ch 6; turn. Skip first 3 sc, sc in next sc, *ch 6, skip next 3 sc, sc in next sc; rep from * across. *4 ch-6 sp.*

Row 3. Ch 4; turn. Sc in first ch-6 sp, *ch 3, sc in next ch-6 sp; rep from * across. Ch 1, dc in bottom of t-ch of previous row. *3 ch-3 sp.*

Row 4. Ch 4; turn. *3 dc in next sc, ch 1; rep from * across. Dc in 3rd ch of t-ch. *13 dc.*

Row 5. Ch 1; turn. *Sc in next ch-sp, ch 6; rep from * across. Sc in 3rd ch of t-ch. *4 ch-6 sp.*

Rows 6-12, (6-12, 6-15, 6-18, 6-21, 6-24, 6-27, 6-30, 6-33). Rep rows 3-5.

Rows 13-14 (13-14, 16-17, 19-20, 22-23, 25-26, 28-29, 31-32, 34-35). Rep rows 3-4.

Row 15 (15, 18, 21, 24, 27, 30, 33, 36). Ch 6; turn. Skip first ch-1 sp, sc in next ch-1 sp, (ch 6, sc in next ch-1 sp) twice, ch 3, dc in t-ch. *3 ch-6 sp.*

Row 16 (16, 19, 22, 25, 28, 31, 34, 37). Ch 1; turn. Sc in dc, *ch 3, sc in next ch-6 sp; rep from * across. *3 ch-3 sp.*

Row 17 (17, 20, 23, 26, 29, 32, 35, 38). Turn. (Sl st, ch 3, 2 dc) in first ch-3 sp, *ch 1, 3 dc in next ch-3 sp; rep from * once. *8 dc and 2 ch-1 sp.*

Row 18 (18, 21, 24, 27, 30, 33, 36, 39). Ch 6; turn. Sc in next ch-1 sp, ch 6, sc in next ch-1 sp, ch 3, dc in t-ch of previous row. *2 ch-6 sp.*

Row 19 (19, 22, 25, 28, 31, 34, 37, 40). Ch 1; turn. Sc in dc, *ch 3, sc in next ch-6 sp; rep from * once. *2 ch-3 sp.*

Row 20 (20, 23, 26, 29, 32, 35, 38, 41). Turn. (Sl st, ch 3, 2 dc) in first ch-3 sp, ch 1, 3 dc in next ch-3 sp. *5 dc and 1 ch-1 sp.*

Row 21 (21, 24, 27, 30, 33, 36, 39, 42). Ch 6; turn. Sc in ch-1 sp, ch 3, dc in t-ch of previous row. *1 ch-6 sp.*

Row 22 (22, 25, 28, 31, 34, 37, 40, 43). Ch 1; turn. Sc in dc, ch 3, sc in ch-6 sp. *1 ch-3 sp.*

Row 23 (23, 26, 29, 32, 35, 38, 41, 44). Turn. (Sl st, ch 3, 2 dc) in ch-3 sp. *2 dc.*

Row 24 (24, 27, 30, 33, 36, 39, 42, 45). Ch 6; turn. Sl st in t-ch of previous row. Finish off.

Right Side Tie

With RS facing, join yarn in top of Row 8 of Right Cup. Ch 1; do not turn.

Row 1. Work 16 sc evenly down first 8 rows of Right Cup. *16 sc.*

Rows 2-24 (2-24, 2-27, 2-30, 2-33, 2-36, 2-39, 2-42, 2-45). Work the same as for Left Side Tie.

Finishing

Make 10 (11, 11, 12, 12, 13, 14, 15, 16) tassels as instructed at the end of the pattern. Attach one tassel with one bead to the end of each top tie and side tie, and one to every other ch-6 sp of the Tassel Belt.

Weave in all ends and trim tassels evenly.

Optional
Sew up bottom 2 (**2**, 4, **4**, 6, **6**, 8, **8**, 8) rows between cups, or as many rows are needed for desired bust coverage.

Hip Scarf

Worked from top to bottom.

Ch 5.

Row 1. Dc in 5th ch from hook (first 4 ch count as 1 dc and 1 ch-1 sp), (ch 1, dc) 4 times in same ch. *6 dc and 5 ch-1 sp.*

Row 2. Ch 3 (counts as dc); turn. 2 dc in first ch-1 sp, ch 1, *3 dc in next ch-1 sp, ch 1; rep from * across. *15 dc and 4 ch-1 sp.*

Row 3. Ch 6; turn. *Skip next dc, sc in next dc, ch 6, skip next dc, sc in next ch-1 sp; rep from * across. Ch 6, skip next dc, sc in next dc, ch 6, sc in last dc. *10 ch-6 sp.*

Row 4. Ch 5; turn. Sc in first ch-6 sp, ch 3, *sc in next ch-6 sp, ch 3; rep from * across, ending last rep with ch 2, dc in bottom of t-ch. *9 ch-3 sp.*

Row 5. Ch 4; turn. 3 dc in first sc, *ch 1, 3 dc in next sc; rep from * across. Ch 1, dc in t-ch. *32 dc.*

Row 6. Ch 6; turn. *Skip next 3 dc, sc in next ch-1 sp, ch 6, skip next dc, sc in next dc, ch 6, skip next dc, sc in next ch-1 sp; rep from * across, working last sc in the t-ch. *15 ch-6 sp.*

Rows 7-8. Rep rows 4-5. *47 dc.*

Row 9. Ch 6; turn. *(Skip next 3 dc, sc in next ch-1 sp, ch 6) twice, skip next dc, sc in next dc, ch 6, skip next dc, sc in next ch-1 sp; rep from * across, working last sc in the t-ch. *20 ch-6 sp.*

Rows 10-11. Rep rows 4-5. *62 dc.*

Row 12. Ch 6; turn. *(Skip next 3 dc, sc in next ch-1 sp, ch 6) 3 times, skip next dc, sc in next dc, ch 6, skip next dc, sc in next ch-1 sp; rep from * across, working last sc in the t-ch. *25 ch-6 sp.*

Rows 13-14. Rep rows 4-5. *77 dc.*

Row 15. Ch 6; turn. *(Skip next 3 dc, sc in next ch-1 sp, ch 6) 4 times, skip next dc, sc in next dc, ch 6, skip next dc, sc in next ch-1 sp; rep from * across, working last sc in the t-ch. *30 ch-6 sp.*

Rows 16-17. Rep rows 4-5. *92 dc.*

Row 18. Ch 6; turn. *(Skip next 3 dc, sc in next ch-1 sp, ch 6) 5 times, skip next dc, sc in next dc, ch 6, skip next dc, sc in next ch-1 sp; rep from * across, working last sc in the t-ch. *35 ch-6 sp.*

Rows 19-20. Rep rows 4-5. *107 dc.*

Row 21. Ch 6; turn. *(Skip next 3 dc, sc in next ch-1 sp, ch 6) 6 times, skip next dc, sc in next dc, ch 6, skip next dc, sc in next ch-1 sp; rep from * across, working last sc in the t-ch. *40 ch-6 sp.*

Rows 22-23. Rep rows 4-5. *122 dc.*

Row 24. Ch 6; turn. *(Skip next 3 dc, sc in next ch-1 sp, ch 6) 7 times, skip next dc, sc in next dc, ch 6, skip next dc, sc in next ch-1 sp; rep from * across, working last sc in the t-ch. *45 ch-6 sp.*

Rows 25-26. Rep rows 4-5. *137 dc.*

Row 27. Ch 6; turn. *(Skip next 3 dc, sc in next ch-1 sp, ch 6) 8 times, skip next dc, sc in next dc, ch 6, skip next dc, sc in next ch-1 sp; rep from * across, working last sc in the t-ch. *50 ch-6 sp.*

Rows 28-29. Rep rows 4-5. *152 dc.*

Sizes S-5X only

Row 30. Ch 6; turn. *(Skip next 3 dc, sc in next ch-1 sp, ch 6) 9 times, skip next dc, sc in next dc, ch 6, skip next dc, sc in next ch-1 sp; rep from * across, working last sc in the t-ch. *55 ch-6 sp.*

Rows 31-32. Rep rows 4-5. *167 dc.*

Sizes M-5X only

Row 33. Ch 6; turn. *(Skip next 3 dc, sc in next ch-1 sp, ch 6) 10 times, skip next dc, sc in next dc, ch 6, skip next dc, sc in next ch-1 sp; rep from * across, working last sc in the t-ch. *60 ch-6 sp.*

Rows 34-35. Rep rows 4-5. *182 dc.*

Sizes L-5X only

Row 36. Ch 6; turn. *(Skip next 3 dc, sc in next ch-1 sp, ch 6) 11 times, skip next dc, sc in next dc, ch 6, skip next dc, sc in next ch-1 sp; rep from * across, working last sc in the t-ch. *65 ch-6 sp.*

Rows 37-38. Rep rows 4-5. *197 dc.*

Sizes 1X-5X only

Row 39. Ch 6; turn. *(Skip next 3 dc, sc in next ch-1 sp, ch 6) 12 times, skip next dc, sc in next dc, ch 6, skip next dc, sc in next ch-1 sp; rep from * across, working last sc in the t-ch. *70 ch-6 sp.*

Rows 40-41. Rep rows 4-5. *212 dc.*

Sizes 2X-5X only

Row 42. Ch 6; turn. *(Skip next 3 dc, sc in next ch-1 sp, ch 6) 13 times, skip next dc, sc in next dc, ch 6, skip next dc, sc in next ch-1 sp; rep from * across, working last sc in the t-ch. *75 ch-6 sp.*

Rows 43-44. Rep rows 4-5. *227 dc.*

Row 45. Ch 6; turn. *(Skip next 3 dc, sc in next ch-1 sp, ch 6) 14 times, skip next dc, sc in next dc, ch 6, skip next dc, sc in next ch-1 sp; rep from * across, working last sc in the t-ch. *80 ch-6 sp.*

Rows 46-47. Rep rows 4-5. *242 dc.*

Sizes 3X-5X only

Row 48. Ch 6; turn. *(Skip next 3 dc, sc in next ch-1 sp, ch 6) 15 times, skip next dc, sc in next dc, ch 6, skip next dc, sc in next ch-1 sp; rep from * across, working last sc in the t-ch. *85 ch-6 sp.*

Rows 49-50. Rep rows 4-5. *257 dc.*

Row 51. Ch 6; turn. *(Skip next 3 dc, sc in next ch-1 sp, ch 6) 16 times, skip next dc, sc in next dc, ch 6, skip next dc, sc in next ch-1 sp; rep from * across, working last sc in the t-ch. *90 ch-6 sp.*

Rows 52-53. Rep rows 4-5. *272 dc.*

Row 54. Ch 6; turn. *(Skip next 3 dc, sc in next ch-1 sp, ch 6) 17 times, skip next dc, sc in next dc, ch 6, skip next dc, sc in next ch-1 sp; rep from * across, working last sc in the t-ch. *95 ch-6 sp.*

Rows 55-56. Rep rows 4-5. *287 dc.*

All Sizes

Row 30 (33, 36, **39,** 42, 48, 51, **51,** 57**).** Ch 6; turn. *Skip next 3 dc, sc next ch-1 sp, ch 6; rep from * across. Sc in t-ch.

Do not finish off.

First Tie

Row 31 (34, 37, **40,** 43, **49,** 52, **52,** 58**).** Ch 4; turn. Sc in first ch-6 sp, *ch 3, sc in next ch-6 sp; rep from * twice. Ch 1, dc in next ch-6 sp. *3 ch-3 sp.*

Row 32 (35, 38, **41,** 44, **50,** 53, **53,** 59**).** Ch 4; turn. *3 dc in next sc, ch 1; rep from * across. Dc in 3rd ch of t-ch. *13 dc.*

Row 33 (36, 39, **42,** 45, **51,** 54, **54,** 60**).** Ch 6; turn. Skip first ch-1 sp, sc in next ch-1 sp, (ch 6, sc in next ch-1 sp) twice, ch 3, dc in t-ch. *3 ch-6 sp.*

Row 34 (37, 40, **43,** 46, **52,** 55, **55,** 61**).** Ch 1; turn. Sc in dc, *ch 3, sc in next ch-6 sp; rep from * across. *3 ch-3 sp.*

Row 35 (38, 41, **44,** 47, **53,** 56, **56,** 62**).** Turn. (Sl st, ch 3, 2 dc) in first ch-3 sp, *ch 1, 3 dc in next ch-3 sp; rep from * once. *8 dc and 2 ch-1 sp.*

Row 36 (39, 42, **45,** 48, **54,** 57, **57,** 63**).** Ch 6; turn. Sc in next ch-1 sp, ch 6, sc in next ch-1 sp, ch 3, dc in t-ch of previous row. *2 ch-6 sp.*

Row 36 (39, 42, **45,** 48, **54,** 57, **57,** 63**).** Ch 1; turn. Sc in dc, *ch 3, sc in next ch-6 sp; rep from * once. *2 ch-3 sp.*

Row 37 (40, 43, **46,** 49, **55,** 58, **58,** 64**).** Turn. (Sl st, ch 3, 2 dc) in first ch-3 sp, ch 1, 3 dc in next ch-3 sp. *5 dc and 1 ch-1 sp.*

Row 38 (41, 44, **47,** 50, **56,** 59, **59,** 65**).** Ch 6; turn. Sc in ch-1 sp, ch 3, dc in t-ch of previous row. *1 ch-6 sp.*

Row 39 (42, 45, **48,** 51, **57,** 60, **60,** 66**).** Ch 1; turn. Sc in dc, ch 3, sc in ch-6 sp. *1 ch-3 sp.*

Row 40 (43, 46, **49,** 52, **58,** 61, **61,** 67**).** Turn. (Sl st, ch 3, 2 dc) in ch-3 sp. *2 dc.*

Row 41 (44, 47, **50,** 53, **59,** 62, **62,** 68**).** Ch 6; turn. Sl st in t-ch of previous row. Finish off.

Second Tie

Join yarn with sl st in opposite corner as first tie.

Row 31 (34, 37, **40,** 43, **49,** 52, **52,** 58**).** Ch 4. Sc in first ch-6 sp, *ch 3, sc in next ch-6 sp; rep from * twice. Ch 1, dc in next ch-6 sp. *3 ch-3 sp.*

Rows 32-41 (35-44, 38-47, **41-50,** 44-53, **50-59,** 53-62, **53-62,** 59-68**).** Work as for same rows of First Tie.

Finishing

Make 27 (**30**, 32, **35**, 37, **42**, 45, **45**, 50) tassels as instructed at the end of the pattern. Attach one tassel with one bead to the end of each tie, and one to every other ch-6 sp of the bottom edge. Weave in all ends and trim tassels evenly.

Gauntlets

Make 2.

Ch 50 (**50**, 54, **58**, 66, **78**, 82, **90**, 94), leaving a 4-inch tail for weaving.

Rnd 1. Dc in 4th ch from hook (first 3 ch count as dc) and next 2 ch, ch 1, skip next ch, *dc in next 3 ch, ch 1, skip next ch; rep from * across, leaving last ch un-worked. Join with sl st in top of t-ch. *36 (36, 39, 42, 48, 57, 60, 66, 69) dc.*

Rnd 2. Ch 1; turn. Sc in first ch, *ch 6, sc in next ch-1 sp; rep from * around to last ch-1 sp. Ch 3, dc in first sc of rnd. *11 (11, 12, 13, 15, 18, 19, 21, 22) ch-6 sp.*

Rnd 3. Ch 3; turn. *Sc in next ch-6 sp, ch 3; rep from * around. Join with sl st in dc of last rnd. *12 (12, 13, 14, 16, 19, 20, 22, 23) ch-3 sp.*

Rnd 4. Ch 3; turn. 2 dc in same dc as joining, ch 1, *3 dc in next sc, ch 1; rep from * around. Join with sl st in top of t-ch. *36 (36, 39, 42, 48, 57, 60, 66, 69) dc.*

Rnd 5. Ch 1; turn. Sc in first ch, *ch 6, sc in next ch-1 sp; rep from * around to last ch-1 sp. Ch 3, sc in first ch-6 sp of rnd. *10 (10, 11, 12, 14, 17, 18, 20, 21) ch-6 sp.*

Rnd 6. Ch 3; turn. *Sc in next ch-6 sp, ch 3; rep from * around. Join with sl st in last sc of last rnd. *11 (11, 12, 13, 15, 18, 19, 21, 22) ch-3 sp.*

Rnd 7. Ch 3; turn. 2 dc in same sc as joining, ch 1, *3 dc in next sc, ch 1; rep from * around. Join with sl st in top of t-ch. *33 (33, 36, 39, 45, 54, 57, 63, 66) dc.*

Rnds 8-31. Rep rnds 2-7. *21 (21, 24, 27, 33, 42, 45, 51, 54) dc.*

Gauntlet is worked in rows from this point forward.

Row 32. Ch 1; turn. Sc in first ch, *ch 6, sc in next ch-1 sp; rep from * once. Ch 3, dc in next ch-1 sp. Leave rem st un-worked. *2 ch-6 sp and 1 ch-3 sp.*

Row 33. Ch 3; turn. Sc in next ch-6 sp, ch 3, sl st in next ch-3 sp. *2 ch-3 sp.*

Row 34. Turn. Sl st in first ch-3 sp, ch 3, 2 dc in same ch-3 sp, ch 1, 3 dc in next ch-3 sp. *6 dc.*

Row 35. Ch 6; turn. Sc in next ch-1 sp, ch 3, dc in t-ch. *1 ch-6 sp and 1 ch-3 sp.*

Row 36. Ch 3; turn. Sl st in next ch-6 sp. *1 ch-3 sp.*

Row 37. Turn. Sl st in first ch-3 sp, ch 3, 2 dc in same ch-3 sp. *3 dc.*

Row 38. Ch 9; turn. Sl st in t-ch. Finger loop made.

Finish off. Weave tail of beg ch through t-ch of rnd 1 to close the gap at the top of the glove. Weave in all rem ends.

Tassels

Set hairpin lace loom to 3 inches. For each tassel, wrap yarn around loom 24 times. Thread a 10-inch length of yarn through the center of the wrapped yarn and tie tightly at on end. Tie a 6-inch length of yarn tightly around the wrapped yarn, about 1 inch down from the tied end. Remove the tassel from the hairpin lace loom. Cut the loops at the bottom of the tassel with sharp scissors.

To attach tassel to costume, thread both ends of the 10-inch yarn up through 1 bead, tie them to indicated ch-6 sp, then thread ends back down through beads and weave into tassel. Trim all ends of tassel evenly.

Layla Amigurumi

This adorable amigurumi would make a wonderful gift for a beloved teacher or friend.

Pattern Level

Intermediate / Intermédiaire / Intermedio

Finished Size
About 7.5" high.

Materials
- Color A: 95 yd 4/worsted-weight yarn
- Color B: 50 yd 4/worsted-weight yarn
- Color C: Scrap 4/worsted-weight yarn
- Color D: Scrap 4/worsted-weight yarn
- 3 yd gold embroidery floss
- Size F-5 (3.75 mm) crochet hook
- 2 15-mm amigurumi eyes
- Polyester fiberfill or stuffing of choice
- Stitch markers
- Yarn needle
- *Optional:* 2 earrings

Note
Unless otherwise indicated, pattern is worked continuously without joining or turning between rounds. To help keep track of your stitches, it may be helpful to place a stitch marker at the beginning of each round.

Eyelashes — make 2.

With Color C, ch 4. Join with sl st to form ring.

Rnd 1. Ch 1, (sc, 2 hdc, picot, hdc, sc, 2 hdc, picot, sc) in ring. Join with sl st to first sc in rnd. Finish off.

Head and Body

With Color A, ch 2.

Rnd 1. 6 sc in second ch from hook. *6 sc.*

Rnd 2. 2 sc in ea sc around. *12 sc.*

Rnd 3. 1 sc in first sc, 2 sc in next sc, *1 sc in next sc, 2 sc in next sc; rep from * around. *18 sc.*

Rnd 4. 1 sc in first 2 sc, 2 sc in next sc, *1 sc in next 2 sc, 2 sc in next sc; rep from * around. *24 sc.*

Rnd 5. 1 sc in first 3 sc, 2 sc in next sc, *1 sc in next 3 sc, 2 sc in next sc; rep from * around. *30 sc.*

Rnd 6. 1 sc in first 4 sc, 2 sc in next sc, *1 sc in next 4 sc, 2 sc in next sc; rep from * around. *36 sc.*

Rnd 7. 1 sc in first 5 sc, 2 sc in next sc, *1 sc in next 5 sc, 2 sc in next sc; rep from * around. *42 sc.*

Rnds 8-13. Sc in ea sc around.

Rnd 14. Dec 1 sc in first 2 sc, sc in next 4 sc, *dec 1 sc in next 2 sc, sc in next 4 sc; rep from * around. *35 sc.*

Rnd 15. Dec 1 sc in first 2 sc, sc in next 3 sc, *dec 1 sc in next 2 sc, sc in next 3 sc; rep from * around. *28 sc.*

Rnd 16. Dec 1 sc in first 2 sc, sc in next 2 sc, *dec 1 sc in next 2 sc, sc in next 2 sc; rep from * around. *21 sc.*

Rnd 17. Dec 1 sc in first 2 sc, sc in next sc, *dec 1 sc in next 2 sc, sc in next sc; rep from * around. Do not finish off. *14 sc.*

Thread post of eyes through beginning ring of eyelashes. Attach amigurumi eyes to head. Stuff head before continuing.

Rnds 18-20. Sc in ea sc around.

Rnd 21. 2 sc in first sc, 1 sc in next sc, *2 sc in next sc, 1 sc in next sc; rep from * around. *21 sc.*

Rnd 22. Sc in ea sc around.

Rnd 23. 2 sc in first sc, sc in next 2 sc, *2 sc in next sc, sc in next 2 sc; rep from * around. *28 sc.*

Rnd 24. Sc in ea sc around.

Rnd 25. Dec 1 sc over first 2 sc, *dec 1 sc over next 2 sc; rep from * around. *14 sc.*

Rnds 26 & 27. Sc in ea sc around.

Rnd 28. Rep rnd 21.

Rnd 29. Rep rnd 23.

Rnd 30. Sc in ea sc around.

Rnd 31. Dec 1 sc over first 2 sc, sc in next 2 sc, *dec 1 sc over next 2 sc, sc in next 2 sc; rep from * around. *21 sc.*

Rnd 32. Dec 1 sc in first 2 sc, sc in next sc, *dec 1 sc in next 2 sc, sc in next sc; rep from * around. *14 sc.*

Stuff body.

Rnd 33. Dec 1 sc in first 2 sc, *dec 1 sc in next 2 sc; rep from * around. Do not finish off. *7 sc.*

Rnd 34. Sl st in ea sc around. Finish off. Weave in all ends.

Ears — make 2.

Worked in rows, from tip to base.

With Color A, ch 2.

Row 1. 3 sc in second ch from hook. *3 sc.*

Row 2. Ch 1; turn. 2 sc in first sc, sc in next sc, 2 sc in last sc. *5 sc.*

Row 3. Ch 1; turn. 2 sc in first sc, sc in next 3 sc, 2 sc in last sc. Do not finish off. *7 sc.*

Rotate ear clockwise and work 2 sc evenly up first side of ear, 3 sc in tip of ear, 2 sc down second side of ear, and 9 sc across bottom of ear. Join with sl st to last sc of row 3; finish off. Weave in all ends.

Muzzle

With Color A, ch 2.

Rnd 1. 6 sc in second ch from hook. *6 sc.*

Rnd 2. 2 sc in ea sc around. *12 sc.*

Rnd 3. Sc in ea sc around; join with sl st to first sc of rnd. Finish off. Weave in all ends.

Embroider nose onto center of muzzle with Color D by first stitching a triangle outline, then filling it in with long, vertical stitches. End with one long, horizontal stitch across the top of the nose.

Arms — make 2

Worked from paw to shoulder.

With Color A, ch 2.

Rnd 1. 6 sc in second ch from hook. *6 sc.*

Rnds 2-11. Sc in ea sc around.

Rnd 12. Sc in ea sc around; join with sl st to first sc in rnd. Finish off. Weave in all ends.

Legs — make 2

Worked from hip to foot.

With Color A, ch 2.

Rnd 1. 6 sc in second ch from hook. *6 sc.*

Rnd 2. 2 sc in ea sc around. *12 sc.*

Rnds 3-11. Sc in ea sc around.

Rnd 12. Sc in first 4 sc, (2 sc in next sc, sc in next sc) three times, sc in last 2 sc. *15 sc.*

Rnds 13-15. Sc in ea sc around.

Finish off.

Paw Pads – make 2.

With Color D, ch 2.

Rnd 1. 6 sc in second ch from hook. *6 sc.*

Rnd 2. 2 sc in ea sc around. *12 sc.*

Rnd 3. Sc in first 4 sc, (2 sc in next sc, sc in next sc) three times, sc in last 2 sc. Finish off. *15 sc.*

Tail

Worked from tip to base.

With Color A, ch 2.

Rnd 1. 6 sc in second ch from hook. *6 sc.*

Rnds 2-17. Sc in ea sc around.

Rnd 18. Sc in ea sc around; join with sl st to first sc in rnd. Finish off. Weave in all ends.

Bra Top

First Cup
With Color B and embroidery floss held together, ch 2.

Rnd 1. 6 sc in second ch from hook. *6 sc.*

Rnd 2. 2 sc in ea sc around. *12 sc.*

Rnd 3. Sc in ea sc around; join with sl st to first sc of rnd. Finish off.

Second Cup
With Color B and embroidery floss held together, ch 2.

Rnd 1. 6 sc in second ch from hook. *6 sc.*

Rnd 2. 2 sc in ea sc around. *12 sc.*

Rnd 3. Sc in ea sc around; join with sl st to first sc of rnd. Sl st in any 2 sc in rnd 3 of First Cup to join. Finish off. Weave in all ends.

Shoulder Straps

Join Color B with sl st in First Cup where strap placement is desired. Ch 12, finish off. Tie knot at end, trim tail. Repeat with Second Cup.

Rib Straps

Join Color B with sl st in First Cup where strap placement is desired. Ch 18, finish off. Tie knot at end, trim tail. Repeat with Second Cup.

Skirt

Worked from waist down.

Belt

With Color B and embroidery floss held together, ch 28.

Row 1. Sc in second ch from hook and ea ch across. *27 sc.*

Row 2. Ch 1; turn. Sc in ea sc across. Finish off.

Right Side

Join Color B with sl st in first unused loop of beg ch of Belt. Ch 3.

Row 1. Working in unused loops of beg ch of Belt, dc in same st as joining, ch 2, skip next 5 ch, (4 dc, ch 2) in next ch, dc in next ch, ch 2, skip next 5 ch, (4 dc, ch 2) in next ch, (dc, ch 2, 4 dc) in next ch; leave rem ch un-worked. *15 dc.*

Row 2. Ch 3; turn. Dc in first dc, skip next ch-2 sp, (4 dc, ch 2, dc, ch 2) in next ch-2 sp, skip next ch-2 sp, (4 dc, ch 2, dc, ch 2) twice in next ch-2 sp, skip next ch-2 sp, 4 dc in top of t-ch. *20 dc.*

Row 3. Ch 3; turn. Dc in first dc, ch 2, *skip next ch-2 sp, (4 dc, ch 2, dc, ch 2) in next ch-2 sp; rep from * across, skip last ch-2 sp, 4 dc in top of t-ch.

Row 4. Ch 3; turn. Dc in first dc, ch 2, skip next ch-2 sp, (4 dc, ch 2, dc, ch 2) in next ch-2 sp, skip next ch-2 sp, (4 dc, ch 2, dc, ch 2) twice in next ch-2 sp, skip next ch-2 sp, (4 dc, ch 2, dc, ch 2) in next ch-2 sp, skip next ch-2 sp, 4 dc in top of t-ch. *25 dc.*

Row 5. Ch 3; turn. Dc in first dc, ch 2, *skip next ch-2 sp, (4 dc, ch 2, dc, ch 2) in next ch-2 sp; rep from * across, skip last ch-2 sp, (4 dc, ch 2, dc, ch 2, 4 dc) in top of t-ch. *30 dc.*

Row 6. Rep row 3. Finish off.

Left Side

Join Color B with sl st in first unused loop of beg ch of Belt. Ch 3.

Row 1. Working in unused loops of beg ch of Belt, dc in same st as joining, ch 2, skip next 5 ch, (4 dc, ch 2) in next ch, dc in next ch, ch 2, skip next 5 ch, (4 dc, ch 2, dc, ch 2, 4 dc) in last ch. *15 dc.*

Rows 2-6. Rep rows 2-6 of Right Side. Finish off. Weave in all ends.

Finishing

Sew ears and muzzle to head. Stuff legs and sew paw pads over openings. Sew arms, legs, and tail to body. Sew back seam of skirt, leaving front slit open. Weave in all ends.

Edging

Join embroidery floss with sl st in any sc on edge of skirt. Sc evenly around skirt, including up and down open slit. Finish off. Weave in all ends.

Rose Garden Zills Pouch and Trainers

This pattern is a must for dancers who play the zills. The pouch keeps your zills together in your dance bag while the trainers keep the sound muffled when practicing in quiet settings.

Pattern Level

Intermediate / Intermédiaire / Intermedio

Finished Sizes
Zills pouch: About 6" square.

Trainers: Fit 2" zills.

Materials

SUPER FINE **MEDIUM**

Zills pouch

- Color A: 95 yd 4/worsted weight yarn
- Color B: Scrap 4/worsted weight yarn
- Color C: Scrap 4/worsted weight yarn
- Size F-5 (3.74 mm) crochet hook
- Stitch markers
- Yarn needle
- Scrap fabric for lining
- Sewing thread in coordinating color
- Sewing needle

Zills Pouch

Front Panel
With Color A, ch 18.

Row 1. Dc in sixth ch from hook, *ch 1, skip next ch, dc in next ch; rep from * across. *7 dc and 6 ch-1 sp.*

Row 2. Ch 4; turn (first 4 ch count as 1 dc and 1 ch-1 sp, now and throughout). Skip first dc and first ch-1 sp, *dc in next dc, ch 1, skip next ch-1 sp; rep from * across. Dc in top of t-ch. *8 dc and 7 ch-1 sp.*

Row 3. Ch 4; turn. Skip first dc and first ch-1 sp, dc in next dc, *ch 1, skip next ch-1 sp, dc in next dc; rep from * across.

Rows 4-7. Rep row 3.

Front is worked in rnds from this point forward.

Rnd 1. Working down end of rows in sp formed by t-ch: (sl st, ch 1, 2 sc) in first sp, *2 sc in ea of next 2 sp, (sc, ch 4, sc) in next sp, 2 sc in ea of next 2 sp*, (2 sc, ch 1, 2 sc) in next sp; corner made. Rep from * around twice. Working across row 7: 2 sc in ea of next 2 ch-1 sp, (sc, ch 4, sc) in next ch-1 sp, 2 sc in ea of next 2 ch-1 sp, 2 sc in next ch-1 sp, ch 1, join with sl st in first sc; beg corner made.

Change to Color B.

Rnd 2. Loosely sl st in next 5 sc, skip next sc, (sc, picot) 5 times in next ch-4 sp, sc in same ch-4 sp, skip next sc, loosely sl st in next 6 sc, *sc in next ch-1 sp; corner made. Loosely sl st in next 6 sc, skip next sc, (sc, picot) 5 times in next ch-4 sp, sc in same ch-4 sp, skip next sc, loosely sl st in next 6 sc; rep from * twice. Sc in next ch-1 sp; corner made. Join with sl st in joining sl st. Finish off.

Join Color A in any corner sc. Ch 1.

Rnd 3. Sc in same sc as joining, ch 5, skip next picot, sl st in next picot, ch 6, skip next picot, sl st in next picot, ch 5, *sc in next corner sc, ch 5, skip next picot, sl st in next picot; ch 6 skip next picot, sl st in next picot, ch 5, rep from * twice. Join with sl st in first sc.

Rnd 4. Ch 1, sc in same sc as joining, 5 sc in next ch-5 sp, sc in next sl st, (4 sc, ch 2, 4 sc) in next ch-6 sp; corner made. Sc in next sl st, 5 sc in next ch-5 sp, *sc in next sc, 5 sc in next ch-5 sp, sc in next sl st, (4 sc, ch 2, 4 sc) in next ch-5 sp; corner made. Sc in next sl st, 5 sc in next ch-5 sp; rep from * twice.

Join with sl st in first sc.

Rnd 5. Ch 1, sc in same sc as joining and next 10 sc, (sc, ch 2, sc) in next ch-2 sp; corner made. *Sc in next 21 sc, (sc, ch 2, sc) in next ch-2 sp; corner made. Rep from * twice. Sc in next 10 sc, join with sl st in first sc. Finish off.

Join Color A with sl st in any corner ch-2 sp.

Rnd 6. Ch 5 (counts as 1 dc and 1 ch-2 sp), dc in same sp as joining; beg corner made. Ch 1, (skip next sc, dc in next sc, ch 1) 11 times, *(dc, ch 2, dc) in next ch-2 sp; corner made. Ch 1, (skip next sc, dc in next sc, ch 1) 11 times; rep from * twice. Join with sl st in third ch of beg ch.

Rnd 7. Ch 1, sc in same ch as joining, 3 sc in next ch-2 sp; corner made. *Working in ea dc and ch-1 sp, sc in next 25 st, 3 sc in next ch-2 sp; corner made. Rep from * twice, sc in next 24 st, join with sl st in first sc. Finish off. Weave in all ends.

Back Panel
Worked exactly as for Front Panel, in Color A only.

Bottom Edge
Bottom Edge is worked through Front Panel and Back Panel together. Join Color A with sl st in bottom corner of both panels.

Row 1. Ch 4, skip next sc, dc in next sc, *ch 1, skip next sc, dc in next sc; rep from * 12 times. *14 ch-1 sp.*

Row 2. Ch 1; turn. Sc in first dc, sc in first ch-1 sp, sc in next dc, skip next ch-1 sp and next dc, dc in next ch-1 sp, (ch 3, dc) 3 times in same ch-1 sp, skip next dc and next ch-1 sp, sc in next dc, skip next ch-1 sp, dc in next dc, *ch 1, skip next ch-1 sp, dc in next dc; rep from * 3 times. Skip next ch-1 sp, sc in next dc, skip next ch-1 sp and next dc, dc in next ch-1 sp, (ch 3, dc) 3 times in same ch-1 sp, skip next dc and next ch-1 sp, sc in next dc, 2 sc in t-ch.

Row 3. Ch 1, turn. Sc in first sc; change to Color C. Skip next 2 sc, (sc, hdc, dc, tr, dc, hdc, sc) in ea of next 3 ch-3 sp, skip next sc; change to Color A. Sc in next dc, skip next ch-1 sp, dc in next dc, ch 1, skip next ch-1 space, dc in next dc, ch 1, skip next ch-1 sp, dc in next dc, skip next ch-1 sp, sc in next dc; change to Color C. (Sc, hdc, dc, tr, dc, hdc, sc) in ea of next 3 ch-3 sp; change to Color A. Skip next sc, sc in last sc. Finish off.

Row 4. Join Color B with sl st in first dc of Color A. Ch 1, sc in same dc as joining, (dc, 2 tr, picot, tr, dc) in next ch-1 sp, sc in next dc, (dc, 2 tr, picot, tr, dc) in next ch-1 sp, sc in next dc. Finish off. Weave in all ends.

Assembly
Sc evenly up sides with Color A.

Top Edge
Worked in rnds.

Join Color A with sl st any sc in top edge.

Rnd 1. Ch 1, sc in same sc as joining, sc 57 evenly around. Join with sl st in first sc. *58 sc.*

Rnd 2. Ch 4, skip first 2 sc, *(dc in next dc, ch 1, skip next sc); rep from * around. Join with sl st in third ch of beg ch-4.

Rnd 3. Ch 1, sc in same ch as joining, sc in ea dc and ch-1 sp around. Join with sl st in first sc.

Rnd 4. Ch 1, sc in same sc as joining, sc in ea sc around. Join with sl st in first sc. Finish off.

Weave in all ends.

Drawstring
With Color A, ch 116. Finish off. Thread in and out of ch-1 sp of rnd 3 of Top Edge. Tie ends of ch together. Trim ends even.

Pouch Lining
Lie pouch flat on fabric to be used for lining. Using pouch as template, cut two panels of fabric around the pouch leaving a .-inch seam allowance. Sew panels together around sides and bottom, leaving top edge open. Sew lining into pouch along top edge.

Trainers — make 2

Note
Pattern is worked continuously without joining or turning between rounds. To help keep track of your stitches, it may be helpful to place a stitch marker at the beginning of each round.

Ch 6; join with sl st in first ch to form ring.

Rnd 1. Ch 3, dc2tog in ring, (ch 3, dc3tog in ring) 5 times, ch 3, join with sl st in top of dc2tog. *1 dc2tog and 5 dc3tog.*

Rnd 2. Sl st in first ch-3 sp, ch 1, sc in same sp, (ch 6, sc in next ch-3 sp) 5 times, ch 3, dc in first sc. *6 ch sp.*

Rnd 3. Ch 4, tr in first sc, ch 1, *dc in next ch-6 sp, ch 1, tr in next sc, ch 1; rep from * around. Join with sl st in third ch of beg ch-4. *6 tr and 6 dc.*

Rnd 4. Ch 1, 2 sc in same ch as joining, sc in first tr, sc in first ch-1 sp, *sc in next dc, sc in next ch-1 sp, sc in next tr, sc in next ch-1 sp; rep from * around. Join with sl st in first sc. Finish off, weave in all ends. *24 sc.*

To muffle sound during practice, place one Trainer over each of the thumb zills.

Valkyrie Bra

This pattern may look intimidating, but it is worked exactly the same as crochet with beading is worked. The key is to make sure all your scales are facing the same way.

Pattern Level

Intermediate / Intermédiaire / Intermedio

Finished Size: XS (**S**, M, **L**, 1X, **2X**, 3X, **4X**, 5X)

Materials:

MEDIUM

- Cascade 220 worsted weight: 1 (**1**, 1, **1**, 2, **2**, 2, **2**, 2) skeins
- Aluminum scales, 7/8 x 1.5 inches: 122 (**140**, 222, **268**, 376, **404**, 570, **644**, 684)
- Size J-10 (6.0mm) crochet hook or size to obtain gauge
- Yarn needle

Gauge Square: Ch 18. *Row 1.* Dc in 4th ch from hook (first 2 ch count as dc) and ea rem ch across. *Row 2.* Ch 3; turn. Dc in ea ch across. *Rows 3-8.* Rep Row 2. Finish off. *16 dc and 8 rows = 4 inches.*

Special Stitch: **Crochet Scale Maille.** Crochet scale maille is worked over a series of two stitches. For counting purposes, both dc and dc2tog are counted as one stitch. When the pattern says to "work in crochet scale maille," you will be adding one scale every two stitches (whether the stitches be dc or dc2tog) as follows:

1. Crochet the first stitch as usual, then carefully remove the hook from the stitch. Thread the loop from the stitch through the hole in the scale, making sure the scale is concave side UP (the scale will be upside down). Replace the loop on the hook.

2. Crochet the second stitch as usual, then remove the hook from the stitch again. Thread the loop through the same scale that was attached in Step 1, flipping the scale in the process so that it is now concave side DOWN. The scale should now be right side up.

3. Repeat steps 1 & 2 for the next two stitches, and so on throughout the scale maille section.

4. If the scale maille section has an uneven number of stitches in any given row, leave the last stitch without a scale.

Note: Pattern is written for smallest size with changes for larger sizes in parentheses. To avoid confusion, it may be helpful to circle the numbers corresponding to your size before beginning this project. When only one number is given, it applies to all sizes.

Special thanks to Lacey Haughawout, Julia Stockert, and Megan White for their help in developing this pattern.

Right Cup

Worked from bottom up.

Ch 142 (**158**, 174, **190**, 206, **222**, 240, **260**, 282).

Row 1 (WS). Dc in 4th ch from hook (first 3 ch count as dc now and throughout pattern) and next 68 (**76**, 84, **92**, 100, **108**, 117, **127**, 138) ch. Leave rem ch un-worked. *70 (78, 86, **94**, 102, **110**, 119, **128**, 140) dc.*

Row 2 (RS). Ch 3; turn. Working in scale maille, dc in next 10 (**11**, 12, **14**, 15, **16**, 18, **20**, 21) dc, 2 dc in ea of next 2 dc, dc in next 11 (**12**, 13, **15**, 16, **17**, 19, **21**, 22) dc; end scale maille section. Dc in next 3 (**3**, 7, **7**, 11, **11**, 15, **15**, 15) dc, dc2tog over next 2 dc, leave rem dc un-worked. *30 (32, 38, 42, 48, 50, 58, 62, 64) st.*

Row 3. Ch 2; turn. Dc in 1st dc (ch 2 and 1st dc count as one dc2tog), dc in ea rem dc across. 29 *(31, 37, 41, 47, 49, 57, 61, 63) dc.*

Sizes XS - S only
Row 4. Ch 3; turn. Working in scale maille, dc in ea dc across to last 3 dc; end scale maille section. Dc in next dc, dc2tog over last 2 dc. 28 *(30, -, -, -, -, -, -) dc.*

Sizes M - L only
Row 4. Ch 3; turn. Working in scale maille, dc in next - (-, 13, **15**, -, -, -, -, -) dc, 2 dc in ea of next 2 dc, dc in next - (-, 14, **16**, -, -, -, -, -) dc; end scale maille section. Dc in next 5 dc, dc2tog over last 2 dc. - *(-, 38, **42**, -, -, -, -, -) dc.*

Row 5. Ch 2; turn. Dc in 1st dc (ch 2 and 1st dc count as one dc2tog), dc in ea rem dc across. - *(-, 37, **41**, -, -, -, -, -) dc.*

Row 6. Ch 3; turn. Working in scale maille, dc in next - (-, 31, **35**, -, -, -, -, -) dc; end scale maille section. Dc in next 3 dc, dc2tog over last 2 dc. - *(-, 36, **40**, -, -, -, -, -) dc.*

Row 7. Rep Row 5. - *(-, 35, **39**, -, -, -, -, -) dc.*

Row 8. Ch 3; turn. Working in scale maille, dc in ea dc across to last 3 dc; end scale maille section. Dc in next dc, dc2tog over last 2 dc. - *(-, 34, **38**, -, -, -, -, -) dc.*

Sizes 1X - 2X only
Row 4. Ch 3; turn. Working in scale maille, dc in next - (-, -, -, 16, **17**, -, -, -) dc, 2 dc in ea of next 2 dc, dc in next - (-, -, -, 17, **18**, -, -, -) dc; end scale maille section. Dc in next 9 dc, dc2tog over last 2 dc. - *(-, -, -, 48, **50**, -, -, -) dc.*

Row 5. Ch 2; turn. Dc in 1st dc (ch 2 and 1st dc count as one dc2tog), dc in ea rem dc across. - *(-, -, -, 47, **49**, -, -, -) dc.*

Row 6. Ch 3; turn. Working in scale maille, dc in next - (-, -, -, 17, **18**, -, -, -) dc, 2 dc in ea of next 2 dc, dc in next - (-, -, -, 18, **19**, -, -, -) dc; end scale maille section. Dc in next 7 dc, dc2tog over last 2 dc. - *(-, -, -, 48, **50**, -, -, -) dc.*

Row 7. Rep Row 5. - *(-, -, -, 47, **49**, -, -, -) dc.*

Row 8. Ch 3; turn. Working in scale maille, dc in next - (-, -, -, 39, **41**, -, -, -) dc; end scale maille section. Dc in next 5 dc, dc2tog over last 2 dc. - *(-, -, -, 46, **48**, -, -, -) dc.*

Row 9. Rep Row 5. - *(-, -, -, 45, **47**, -, -, -) dc.*

Row 10. Ch 3; turn. Working in scale maille, dc in next - (-, -, -, 39, **41**, -, -, -) dc; end scale maille section. Dc in next 3 dc, dc2tog over last 2 dc. - *(-, -, -, 44, **46**, -, -, -) dc.*

Row 11. Rep Row 5. - *(-, -, -, 43, **45**, -, -, -) dc.*

Row 12. Ch 3; turn. Working in scale maille, dc in ea dc across to last 3 dc; end scale maille section. Dc in next dc, dc2tog over last 2 dc. - (-, -, **-**, *42*, **44**, **-**, **-**, -) *dc.*

Sizes 3X - 5X only
Row 4. Ch 3; turn. Working in scale maille, dc in next - (-, -, **-**, -, **-**, 19, **21**, 22) dc, 2 dc in ea of next 2 dc, dc in next - (-, -, **-**, -, **-**, 20, **22**, 23) dc; end scale maille section. Dc in next 13 dc, dc2tog over last 2 dc. - (-, -, **-**, -, **-**, *58*, **62**, *64*) *dc.*

Row 5. Ch 2; turn. Dc in 1st dc (ch 2 and 1st dc count as one dc2tog), dc in ea rem dc across. - (-, -, **-**, -, **-**, *57*, **61**, *63*) *dc.*

Row 6. Ch 3; turn. Working in scale maille, dc in next - (-, -, -, -, **-**, 20, **22**, 23) dc, 2 dc in ea of next 2 dc, dc in next - (-, -, -, -, **-**, 21, **23**, 24) dc; end scale maille section. Dc in next 11 dc, dc2tog over last 2 dc. - (-, -, **-**, -, **-**, *58*, **62**, *64*) *dc.*

Row 7. Rep Row 5. - (-, -, **-**, -, **-**, *57*, **61**, *63*) *dc.*

Row 8. Ch 3; turn. Dc in next - (-, -, -, -, -, 21, **23**, 24) dc, 2 dc in ea of next 2 dc, dc in next - (-, -, -, -, **-**, 22, **24**, 25) dc; end scale maille section. Dc in next 9 dc, dc2tog over last 2 dc. - (-, -, **-**, -, **-**, *58*, **62**, *64*) *dc.*

Row 9. Rep Row 5. (-, -, **-**, -, **-**, *57*, **61**, *63*) *dc.*

Row 10. Ch 3; turn. Dc in next - (-, -, -, -, -, 47, **51**, 53) dc; end scale maille section. Dc in next 7 dc, dc2tog over last 2 dc. - (-, -, **-**, -, **-**, *56*, **60**, *62*) *dc.*

Row 11. Rep Row 5. - (-, -, **-**, -, **-**, *55*, **59**, *61*) *dc.*

Row 12. Ch 3; turn. Dc in next - (-, -, -, -, -, 47, **51**, 53) dc; end scale maille section. Dc in next 5 dc, dc2tog over last 2 dc. - (-, -, **-**, -, **-**, *54*, **58**, *60*) *dc.*

Row 13. Rep Row 5. - (-, -, **-**, -, **-**, *53*, **57**, *59*) *dc.*

Row 14. Ch 3; turn. Dc in next - (-, -, -, -, **-**, 47, **51**, 53) dc; end scale maille section. Dc in next 3 dc, dc2tog over last 2 dc. - (-, -, **-**, -, **-**, *52*, **56**, *58*) *dc.*

Row 15. Rep Row 5. - (-, -, **-**, -, **-**, *51*, **55**, *57*) *dc.*

Row 16. Ch 3; turn. Working in scale maille, dc in ea dc across to last 3 dc; end scale maille section. Dc in next dc, dc2tog over last 2 dc. - (-, -, **-**, -, **-**, *50*, **54**, *56*) *dc.*

All Sizes
Row 5 (5, *9,* **9,** *13,* **13,** *17,* **17,** *17*). Ch 2; turn. Dc in 1st dc (ch 2 and 1st dc count as one dc2tog), dc in next 7 (**8,** *7,* **9,** *8,* **9,** *9,* **11,** *12*) dc, (dc2tog over next 2 dc, dc in next dc) 2 (**2,** *4,* **4,** *6,* **6,** *8,* **8,** *8*) times, dc in ea rem dc across to last 3 dc, dc2tog over next 2 dc, dc in last dc. *24 (26, 28, 32, 34, 36,* **40,** *44, 46*) *dc.*

Row 6 (6, *10,* **10,** *14,* **14,** *18,* **18,** *18*). Ch 3; turn. Working in scale maille, dc2tog over next 2 dc, dc in ea rem dc across to last 3 dc, dc2tog over next 2 dc, dc in last dc. End scale maille section. *22 (24, 26,* **30,** *32, 34, 38, 42, 44*) *dc.*

Row 7 (7, *11,* **11,** *15,* **15,** *19,* **19,** *19*). Ch 2; turn. Dc in 1st dc (ch 2 and 1st dc count as one dc2tog), dc in ea rem dc across to last 3 dc, dc2tog over next 2 dc, dc in last dc. *20 (22, 24, 28, 30,* **32,** *36,* **40,** *42*) *dc.*

Row 8 (8, *12,* **12,** *16,* **16,** *20,* **20,** *20*). Ch 3; turn. Working in scale maille, dc2tog over next 2 dc, dc in ea rem dc across to last 3 dc, dc2tog over next 2 dc, dc in last dc. End scale maille section. *18 (20, 22, 26, 28,* **30,** *34, 38, 40*) *dc.*

Sizes X-Small, Medium, Large, 2X, 3X, and 4X

Rows 9-14 (-, 13-20, **13-22,** -, **17-28,** 21-34, **21-36,** -**).** Rep previous 2 rows, adding only 1 scale in the last row. *5 dc.*

Row 15 (-, 21, **23,** -, **29,** 35, **37,** -**).** Ch 2; turn. Dc in 1st dc (ch 2 and 1st dc count as one dc2tog), dc in ea rem dc across to last 3 dc, dc2tog over next 2 dc, dc in last dc. *4 dc.*

Row 16 (-, 22, **24,** -, **30,** 36, **38,** -**).** Ch 3; turn. Dc in ea dc across, adding 1 scale in the middle of the row.

Sizes Small, 1X, and 5X

Rows - (7-16, -, -, **17-28,** -, -, -, **21-38).** Rep previous 2 rows. *4 dc.*

Row - (17, -, -, **29,** -, -, -, **39).** Ch 3; turn. Dc in ea dc across.

Row - (18, -, -, **30,** -, -, -, **40).** Ch 3; turn. Dc in ea dc across, adding 1 scale in the middle of the row.

All Sizes

Rows 17-42 (19-45, 23-52, **25-58,** 31-67, **31-70,** 37-78, **39-80,** 41-81**).** Ch 3; turn. Dc in ea dc across.

Finish off.

Left Cup

Worked from bottom up.

Left Cup is worked in un-worked ch of beg ch from Right Cup. With WS facing and leaving a long tail for sewing later, join yarn with sl st in first un-worked ch. Ch 3 (counts as dc); *do not turn.*

Row 1. Dc in ea rem un-worked ch across. Finish off.

Row 2. With RS facing, skip first 40 (**46,** 48, **52,** 54, **60,** 61, **66,** 76) dc, ch 2, dc in first dc (ch 2 and 1st dc count as one dc2tog), dc in next 3 (**3,** 7, **7,** 11, **11,** 15, **15,** 15) dc; begin scale maille section. Dc in next 11 (**12,** 13, **15,** 16, **17,** 19, **21,** 22) dc, 2 dc in ea of next 2 dc, dc in ea rem dc across. End scale maille section. *30 (32, 38, 42, 48, 50, 58, 62, 64) st.*

Row 3. Ch 3; turn. Dc in ea dc across to last 2 st, dc2tog over last 2 st. 29 *(31, 37, 41, 47, 49, 57, 61, 63) dc.*

Sizes XS - S only

Row 4. Ch 2, dc in next dc (ch 2 and 1st dc count as one dc2tog), dc in next dc; begin scale maille section. Dc in ea rem dc across. 28 *(30, -, -, -, -, -, -, -) dc.*

Sizes M - L only

Row 4. Ch 2, dc in next dc (ch 2 and 1st dc count as one dc2tog), dc in next 5 dc; begin scale maille section. Dc in next - (-, 14, **16,** -, -, -, -, -) dc, 2 dc in ea of next 2 dc, dc in ea rem dc across. End scale maille section. *- (-, 38, 42, -, -, -, -, -) dc.*

Row 5. Ch 3; turn. Dc in ea dc across to last 2 st, dc2tog over last 2 st. *- (-, 37, 41, -, -, -, -, -) dc.*

Row 6. Ch 2, dc in next dc (ch 2 and 1st dc count as one dc2tog), dc in next 3 dc; begin scale maille section. Dc in ea rem dc across. *- (-, 36, 40, -, -, -, -, -) dc.*

Row 7. Rep Row 5. *- (-, 35, 39, -, -, -, -, -) dc.*

Row 8. Ch 2, dc in next dc (ch 2 and 1st dc count as one dc2tog), dc in next dc; begin scale maille section. Dc in ea rem dc across. *- (-, 34, 38, -, -, -, -, -) dc.*

Sizes 1X - 2X only

Row 4. Ch 2, dc in next dc (ch 2 and 1st dc count as one dc2tog), dc in next 9 dc; begin scale maille section. Dc in next - (-, -, -, 17, **18**, -, -, -) dc, 2 dc in ea of next 2 dc, dc in ea rem dc across. End scale maille section. - (-, -, -, 48, **50**, -, **-**, -) dc.

Row 5. Ch 3; turn. Dc in ea dc across to last 2 st, dc2tog over last 2 st. - (-, -, **-**, 47, **49**, -, **-**, -) dc.

Row 6. Ch 2, dc in next dc (ch 2 and 1st dc count as one dc2tog), dc in next 7 dc; begin scale maille section. Dc in next - (-, -, -, 18, **19**, -, **-**, -) dc, 2 dc in ea of next 2 dc, dc in ea rem dc across. End scale maille section. - (-, -, **-**, 48, **50**, -, **-**, -) dc.

Row 7. Rep Row 5. - (-, -, **-**, 47, **49**, -, **-**, -) dc.

Row 8. Ch 2, dc in next dc (ch 2 and 1st dc count as one dc2tog), dc in next 5 dc; begin scale maille section. Dc in ea rem dc across. End scale maille section. - (-, -, **-**, 46, **48**, -, **-**, -) dc.

Row 9. Rep Row 5. - (-, -, **-**, 45, **47**, -, **-**, -) dc.

Row 10. Ch 2, dc in next dc (ch 2 and 1st dc count as one dc2tog), dc in next 3 dc; begin scale maille section. Dc in ea rem dc across. End scale maille section. - (-, -, **-**, 44, **46**, -, **-**, -) dc.

Row 11. Rep Row 5. - (-, -, **-**, 43, **45**, -, **-**, -) dc.

Row 12. Ch 2, dc in next dc (ch 2 and 1st dc count as one dc2tog), dc in next dc; begin scale maille section. Dc in ea rem dc across. - (-, -, **-**, 42, **44**, -, **-**, -) dc.

Sizes 3X - 5X only

Row 4. Ch 2, dc in next dc (ch 2 and 1st dc count as one dc2tog), dc in next 13 dc; begin scale maille section. Dc in next - (**-**, -, **-**, -, **-**, 20, **22**, 23) dc, 2 dc in ea of next 2 dc, dc in ea rem dc across. End scale maille section. - (-, **3** -, **-**, -, **-**, 58, **62**, 64) dc.

Row 5. Ch 3; turn. Dc in ea dc across to last 2 st, dc2tog over last 2 st. - (**-**, -, **-**, -, **-**, 57, **61**, 63) dc.

Row 6. Ch 2, dc in next dc (ch 2 and 1st dc count as one dc2tog), dc in next 11 dc; begin scale maille section. Dc in next - (-, -, -, -, **-**, 21, **23**, 24) dc, 2 dc in ea of next 2 dc, dc in ea rem dc across. End scale maille section. - (-, -, **-**, -, **-**, 58, **62**, 64) dc.

Row 7. Rep Row 5. - (-, -, **-**, -, **-**, 57, **61**, 63) dc.

Row 8. Ch 2, dc in next dc (ch 2 and 1st dc count as one dc2tog), dc in next 9 dc; begin scale maille section. Dc in next - (-, -, -, -, **-**, 22, **24**, 25) dc, 2 dc in ea of next 2 dc, dc in ea rem dc across. End scale maille section. - (-, -, **-**, -, **-**, 58, **62**, 64) dc.

Row 9. Rep Row 5. - (-, -, **-**, -, **-**, 57, **61**, 63) dc.

Row 10. Ch 2, dc in next dc (ch 2 and 1st dc count as one dc2tog), dc in next 7 dc; begin scale maille section. Dc in ea rem dc across. End scale maille section. - (-, -, **-**, -, **-**, 56, **60**, 62) dc.

Row 11. Rep Row 5. - (-, -, **-**, -, **-**, 55, **59**, 61) dc.

Row 12. Ch 2, dc in next dc (ch 2 and 1st dc count as one dc2tog), dc in next 5 dc; begin scale maille section. Dc in ea rem dc across. End scale maille section. - (-, -, **-**, -, **-**, 54, **58**, 60) dc.

Row 13. Rep Row 5. - (-, -, **-**, -, **-**, 53, **57**, 59) dc.

Row 14. Ch 2, dc in next dc (ch 2 and 1st dc count as one dc2tog), dc in next 3 dc; begin scale maille section. Dc in ea rem dc across. End scale maille section. - (-, -, **-**, -, **-**, 52, **56**, 58) dc.

Row 15. Rep Row 5. - *(-, -, -, -, -, 51, 55, 57) dc.*

Row 16. Ch 2, dc in next dc (ch 2 and 1st dc count as one dc2tog), dc in next dc; begin scale maille section. Dc in ea rem dc across. - *(-, -, -, -, -, 50, 54, 56) dc.*

All Sizes
Rows 5-42 (5-45, 9-52, **9-58,** 13-67, **13-70,** 17-78, **17-80,** 17-81**).** Work the same as for Right Cup.

Finish off.

Finishing

Optional: Sew up bottom 4 (**4,** 8, **8,** 12, **12,** 16, **16,** 16) rows between cups, or as many rows are needed for desired bust coverage.

Bird of Paradise Halter and Skirt

This pattern was named for the pineapple design of the skirt, which always reminded me of a male peacock's tail. The stitch pattern of the matching halter was chosen to invoke the texture of the peacock's blue feathers.

Pattern Level

Complex / Complexe / Complejo

Finished Size

Women's XS (**S**, M, **L**, 1X, **2X**, 3X, **4X**, 5X)

Materials

MEDIUM

- Cascade Casablanca, 3 (**3**, 4, **4**, 4, **5**, 5, **5**, 6) skeins
- 3 half-inch buttons
- Size J-10 (6.0mm) crochet hook or size to obtain gauge
- Yarn needle
- *Optional:* 3 stitch markers

Gauge Square

Row 1. Ch 26. Sc in second ch from hook and next ch, *skip next 2 ch, 5 dc in next ch, *skip next 2 ch, sc in next 3 ch, skip next 2 ch, 5 dc in next ch; rep from * once. Skip next 2 ch, sc in last 2 ch.

Row 2. Ch 4; turn. (Dc, ch 1) in first sc, *skip next sc and dc, sc in next 3 dc, ch 1, skip next dc and sc, ch 1, (dc, ch 1) twice in next sc; rep from * across.

Row 3. Ch 3; turn. 2 dc in first ch-1 sp, sc in next 3 sc, *5 dc in next ch-1 sp, sc in next 3 sc; rep from * across. 3 dc in t-ch.

Row 4. Ch 1; turn. Sc in first 2 dc, ch 1, skip next dc and sc, (dc, ch 1) twice in next sc, skip next sc and dc, *sc in next 3 dc, ch 1, skip next dc and sc, (dc, ch 1) twice in next sc, skip next sc and dc; rep from * across. Sc in next dc and t-ch.

Row 5. Ch 1; turn. Sc in first 2 sc, skip next ch-1 sp, 5 dc in next ch-1 sp, *skip next ch-1 sp, sc in next 3 sc, skip next ch-1 sp, 5 dc in next ch-1 sp; rep from * across. Skip next ch-1 sp, sc in last 2 sc.

Rows 6-9. Rep rows 2-5. Finish off.

Gauge square should measure about 5 inches square.

Special Stitches

Shell Foundation. (Ch 1, dc, ch 1, dc, ch 1) in second sc of 3-sc group *or* middle sc of Shell Dart.

Shell. 5 dc in middle ch-1 sp of Shell Foundation.

Shell Dart Foundation. (Dc, ch 1, dc, ch 1, dc) in second sc of 3-sc group OR middle sc of Shell Dart.

Shell Dart. Working in Shell Dart Foundation, 5 dc in first ch-1 sp, sc in middle dc, 5 dc in second ch-1 sp.

3-sc Group. Sc in next 3 dc.

Pineapple Shell. (3 dc, ch 3, 3 dc) in indicated ch-sp. When instructions are given to work a pineapple

shell in another pineapple shell, it is worked in the ch-3 sp.

Note

Pattern is written for smallest size with changes for larger sizes in parentheses. To avoid confusion, it may be helpful to circle the numbers corresponding to your size before beginning this project. When only one number is given, it applies to all sizes.

Halter

Worked from top down.

Ch 26.

Row 1 (WS). Sc in second ch from hook and next ch, *skip next 2 ch, 5 dc in next ch, *skip next 2 ch, sc in next 3 ch, skip next 2 ch, 5 dc in next ch; rep from * once. Skip next 2 ch, sc in last 2 ch. *3 shells.*

Note

Even-numbered rows are the **foundation rows**, are worked in back loops only (blo), and are the RS of the halter. Odd-numbered rows are the **shell rows**, worked in both loops, and are the WS of the halter.

Row 2 (blo). Ch 4; turn. (Dc, ch 1) in first sc, *skip next sc and dc, sc in next 3 dc, ch 1, skip next dc and sc, ch 1, (dc, ch 1) twice in next sc; rep from * across.

Row 3. Ch 3; turn. 4 dc in first ch-1 sp, *sc in next 3 sc, skip next ch-1 sp, 5 dc in next ch-1 sp; rep from * across. *4 shells.*

Row 4 (blo). Ch 4; turn. (Dc, ch 1) in first dc, sc in next 3 dc (3-sc group made), ch 1, *skip next dc and sc, ch 1 (dc, ch 1) twice in next sc (Shell Foundation made), skip next sc and dc, sc in next 3 dc; rep from * across. (Dc, ch 1, dc) in t-ch.

Row 5. Ch 3; turn. 4 dc in first ch-1 sp, *sc in next 3 sc (3-sc group made), skip next ch-1 sp, 5 dc in next ch-1 sp (shell made); rep from * across. *5 shells.*

Rows 6-13 (6-11, 6-11, **6-11,** 6-9, **6-9,** 6-9, **6-9,** 6-9**).** Rep rows 4 & 5. *9 (8, 8, 8, 7, 7, 7, 7, 7) shells.*

Sizes S-5X only
Rows - (12-13, 12-13, **12-13,** 10-13, **10-13,** 10-13, **10-13,** 10-13**).** Rep rows 4 & 5, replacing Shell Foundations and Shells with Shell Dart Foundations and Shell Darts as indicated in the Bust Shaping diagram at the end of the pattern. - *(10, 12, 13, 15, 17, 19, 21, 23) shells.*

Row 14 (blo). Rep row 4, working a Shell Foundation into the middle sc of each Shell Dart.

Row 15. Rep row 5. - *(11, 13, **14**, 16, **18**, 20, **22**, 24) shells.*

All Sizes
Rows 14-23 (16-23, 16-23, **16-25,** 16-25, **16-25,** 16-25, **16-25,** 16-25**).** Rep rows 4 & 5. *14 (15, 17, **19**, 21, **23**, 25, **27**, 29) shells.*

Row 24 (24, 24, **26,** 26, **26,** 26, **26,** 26**) (blo).** Rep row 4.

Row 25 (25, 25, **27,** 27, **27,** 27, **27,** 27**).** Ch 3; turn. 2 dc in first ch-1 sp, sc in next 3 sc, *5 dc in next ch-1 sp, sc in next 3 sc; rep from * across. 3 dc in t-ch. *13 (**14**, 16, **18**, 20, **22**, 24, **26**, 28) shells and 2 half-shells.*

Row 26 (26, 26, **28,** 28, **28,** 28, **28,** 28**) (blo).** Ch 3; turn. Sc in first dc; buttonhole made. Sc in next dc, ch 1, skip next dc and sc, (dc, ch 1) twice in next sc, skip next sc and dc, *sc in next 3 dc, ch 1, skip next dc and sc, (dc, ch 1) twice in next sc, skip next sc and dc; rep from * across. Sc in next dc and t-ch.

Optional
Place a stitch marker on the buttonhole so you can easily see it as subsequent rows are worked.

Row 27 (27, 27, **29,** 29, **29,** 29, **29,** 29**).** Ch 1; turn. Sc in first 2 sc, skip next ch-1 sp, 5 dc in next ch-1 sp, *skip next ch-1 sp, sc in next 3 sc, skip next ch-1 sp, 5 dc in next ch-1 sp; rep from * across. Skip next ch-1 sp, sc in last 2 sc. *14 (**15**, 17, **19**, 21, **23**, 25, **27**, 29) shells.*

Row 28 (28, 28, **30,** 30, **30,** 30, **30,** 30**) (blo).** Ch 4; turn. (Dc, ch 1) in first sc, skip next sc and dc, sc in next 3 dc, ch 1, *skip next dc and sc, (dc, ch 1)

twice in next sc, skip next sc and dc, sc in next 3 dc ch 1; rep from * across. Skip next dc and sc, (dc, ch 1, dc) in last sc.

Rows 29-36 (29-36, 29-36, **31-38,** 31-38, **31-38,** 31-38, **31-38,** 31-38**).** Rep previous 4 rows.

Row 37 (37, 37, **39,** 39, **39,** 39, **39,** 39**).** Rep row 25 (**25,** 25, **27,** 27, **27,** 27, **27,** 27). Finish off.

Ties
With RS facing, join yarn with sl st in upper right corner. Ch 51, sc in second ch from hook and ea ch across, continue with 25 sc evenly across top of Halter, ch 51, sc in second ch from hook and ea rem ch, join with sl st in upper left corner of Halter. Finish off.

Finishing
Sew buttons on the opposite edge as buttonholes in the rows that align with the buttonholes.

Skirt

Worked from top to bottom.

Ch 128 (**128**, 146, **164**, 182, **200**, 200, **200**, 218), leaving a 6-inch tail for weaving.

Rnd 1. Sc in second ch from hook, ch 1, skip next ch, sc in next 2 sc, ch 3, skip next 2 ch, sc in next 2 ch, *ch 3, skip next 3 ch, sc in next 2 ch, ch 3, skip next 2 ch, sc in next 2 ch; rep from * across to last 2 ch. Ch 1, skip next ch, sc in last ch. Join with sl st in first sc in rnd.

Rnd 2. Ch 3; turn. Sc in first ch-sp, ch 3, 3 dc in next ch-sp, ch 4, sc in next ch-sp, *ch 4, 3 dc in next ch-sp, (ch 3, 3 dc in next ch-sp) twice, ch 4, sc in next ch-sp; rep from * across to last 2 ch-sp. Ch 4, 3 dc in next ch-sp, ch 3, dc in last ch-sp, dc in last sc. Join with sl st in top of t-ch.

Rnd 3. Ch 6; turn. 3 dc in first ch-sp, ch 3, sc in next ch-sp, *ch 5, sc in next ch-sp, ch 3, 3 dc in next ch-sp, ch 5, 3 dc in next ch-sp, ch 3, sc in next ch-sp; rep from * across to last 2 ch-sp. Ch 5, sc in next ch-sp, ch 3, 3 dc in last ch-sp, ch 2, tr in t-ch of previous rnd. Join with sl st fourth ch of t-ch of current rnd.

Rnd 4. Ch 1; turn. Sc in tr, ch 6, skip first ch-sp, 3 dc in next ch-sp, ch 3, sc in next ch-sp, *ch 3, 3 dc in next ch-sp, ch 6, sc in next ch-sp, ch 6, 3 dc in next ch-sp, ch 3, sc in next ch-sp; rep from * across to last ch-sp. Ch 3, 3 dc in last ch-sp, ch 6, sc in t-ch of previous rnd. Join with sl st in first sc in rnd.

Rnd 5. Ch 7; turn. Sc in first ch-sp, ch 5, *3 dc in next ch-sp, ch 3, 3 dc in next ch-sp, ch 5, sc in next ch-sp, ch 6, sc in next ch-sp, ch 5; rep from * across to last 3 ch-sp. 3 dc in next ch-sp, ch 3, 3 dc in next ch-sp, ch 5, sc in next ch-sp, ch 3, tr in last sc. Join with sl st in fourth ch of t-ch of current rnd.

Rnd 6. Ch 5; turn. (Tr, ch 1) twice in first ch-sp, sc in next ch-sp, ch 3, pineapple shell in next ch-sp, *ch 3, sc in next ch-sp, ch 1, (tr, ch 1) 5 times in next ch-sp, sc in next ch-sp, ch 3, pineapple shell in next ch-sp; rep from * across to last ch-sp. Ch 3, sc in last ch-sp, (ch 1, tr) 3 times in top of t-ch of previous rnd. Join with sl st in fourth ch of t-ch of current rnd.

Rnd 7. Ch 1; turn. Sc in first tr, (ch 3, sc in next tr) twice, ch 3, pineapple shell in next pineapple shell, *(ch 3, sc in next tr) 5 times, ch 3, pineapple shell in next pineapple shell; rep from * across until last pineapple shell is worked. Ch 3, (sc in next tr, ch 3) twice, sc in fourth ch of t-ch of previous rnd. Join with sl st in first sc of current rnd.

Rnd 8. Ch 3; turn. Sc in first ch-sp, ch 3, sc in next ch-sp, ch 3, pineapple shell in next pineapple shell, *ch 3, skip next ch-sp, (sc in next ch-sp, ch 3) 4 times, pineapple shell in next pineapple shell; rep from * across until last pineapple shell is worked. Ch 3, skip next ch-sp, sc in next ch-sp, ch 3, sc in next ch-sp, ch 1, hdc in last sc. Join with sl st in second ch of t-ch of current rnd.

Rnd 9. Ch 1; turn. Sc in hdc, ch 3, skip ch-1 sp, sc in next ch-sp, ch 3, (3 dc, ch 3, dc, ch 3, 3 dc) in next pineapple shell, *ch 3, skip next ch-sp, (sc in next ch-sp, ch 3) 3 times, skip next ch-sp, (3 dc, ch 3, dc, ch 3, 3 dc) in next pineapple shell; rep from * across until last pineapple shell is worked. Ch 3, skip next ch-sp, sc in next ch-sp, ch 3, sc in top of t-ch of previous rnd. Join with sl st in first sc of current rnd.

Rnd 10. Ch 3; turn. Sc in first ch-sp, ch 3, skip next ch-sp, (pineapple shell in next ch-sp) twice, *ch 3, skip next ch-sp, (sc in next ch-sp, ch 3) twice, skip next ch-sp, (pineapple shell in next ch-sp) twice; rep from * across to last 2 ch-sp. Ch 3, skip next ch-sp, sc in last ch-sp, ch 1, hdc in last sc. Join with sl st in second ch of t-ch of current rnd.

Rnd 11. Ch 1; turn. Sc in hdc, ch 3, pineapple shell in next pineapple shell, *ch 5, pineapple shell in next pineapple shell, ch 3, skip next ch-sp, sc in next ch-sp, ch 3, pineapple shell in next pineapple shell; rep from * across until 1 pineapple shell remains. Ch 5, pineapple shell in last pineapple shell, ch 3, sc in second ch of t-ch of previous rnd. Join with sl st in first sc of current rnd.

Rnd 12. Ch 6; turn. Skip first ch-sp, (dc, ch 3, 3 dc) in next pineapple shell, ch 6, sc in next ch-sp, *ch 6, (3 dc, ch 3, dc) in next pineapple shell, (dc, ch 3, 3 dc) in next pineapple shell, ch 6, sc in next ch-sp; rep from * across to last 2 ch-sp. Ch 6, (3 dc, ch 3, dc) in next ch-sp, skip last ch-sp, trtr in last sc in rnd. Join with sl st in first dc of current rnd.

Rnd 13. Ch 5; turn. 3 dc in first ch-sp, ch 5, sc in next ch-sp, *ch 6, sc in next ch-sp, ch 5, 3 dc in next ch-sp, ch 3, 3 dc in next ch-sp, ch 5, sc in next ch-sp; rep from * across to last 2 ch-sp. Ch 6, sc in next ch-sp, ch 5, 3 dc in last ch-sp, ch 1, tr in last dc. Join with sl st in fourth ch of t-ch of current rnd.

Row 14. Ch 3; turn. 2 dc in first ch-1 sp, ch 3, sc in next ch-5 sp, (ch 1, tr) 5 times in next ch-6 sp, ch 1, sc in next ch-5 sp,* ch 3, pineapple shell in next ch-3 sp, ch 3, sc in next ch-5 sp, (ch 1, tr) 5 times in next ch-6 sp, ch 1, sc in next ch-5 sp; rep from * across. Ch 3, 3 dc in top of t-ch. *Do not join between rows from this point forward.*

Row 15. Ch 3; turn. 2 dc in first dc, ch 3, (sc in next tr, ch 3) 5 times, *pineapple shell in next pineapple shell, ch 3, (sc in next tr, ch 3) 5 times; rep from * across. 3 dc in t-ch.

Row 16. Ch 3; turn. 2 dc in first dc, skip next ch-sp, (sc in next ch-sp, ch 3) 4 times, *skip next ch-sp, pineapple shell in next pineapple shell, skip next ch-sp, (sc in next ch-sp, ch 3) 4 times; rep from * across. 3 dc in t-ch.

Row 17. Ch 3; turn. 2 dc in first dc, skip next ch-sp, (sc in next ch-sp, ch 3) 3 times, *skip next ch-sp, (3 dc, ch 3, dc, ch 3, 3 dc) in next pineapple shell, skip next ch-sp, (sc in next ch-sp, ch 3) 3 times; rep from * across. 3 dc in t-ch.

Row 18. Ch 3; turn. 2 dc in first dc, skip next ch-sp, (sc in next ch-sp, ch 3) twice, *skip next ch-sp, pineapple shell in ea of next 2 ch-sp, skip next ch-sp, (sc in next ch-sp, ch 3) twice; rep from * across. 3 dc in t-ch.

Row 19. Ch 3; turn. 2 dc in first dc, skip next ch-sp, sc in next ch-sp, ch 3, *skip next ch-sp, pineapple shell in next pineapple shell, ch 5, pineapple shell in next pineapple shell, skip next ch-sp, sc in next ch-sp, ch 3; rep from * across. 3 dc in t-ch.

Row 20. Ch 2; turn. (Dc, ch 3, 3 dc) in first pineapple shell, ch 6, sc in next ch-sp, ch 6, (3 dc, ch 3) in next pineapple shell. *Dc2tog, working first dc in same shell as last st and second dc in next pineapple shell. Ch 3, 3 dc in same pineapple shell as last st, ch 6, sc in next ch-sp, ch 6, (3 dc, ch 3) in next pineapple shell; rep from * across. Dc2tog, working first dc in same pineapple shell as last st and second dc in t-ch.

Row 21. Ch 3; turn. 2 dc in first ch-sp, ch 5, sc in next ch-sp, ch 6, sc in next ch-sp, ch 5, 3 dc in next ch-sp, *ch 3, 3 dc in next ch-sp, ch 5, sc in next ch-sp, ch 6, sc in next ch-sp, ch 5, 3 dc in next ch-sp; rep from * across.

Row 22. Ch 3; turn. 2 dc in first dc, ch 3, sc in next ch-5 sp, (ch 1, tr) 5 times in next ch-6 sp, ch 1, sc in next ch-5 sp,* ch 3, pineapple shell in next ch-3 sp, ch 3, sc in next ch-5 sp, (ch 1, tr) 5 times in next ch-6 sp, ch 1, sc in next ch-5 sp; rep from * across. Ch 3, 3 dc in top of t-ch.

Rows 23 & 24. Rep rows 15 & 16.

Row 25 (RS). Ch 3; turn. 2 dc in first dc, skip next ch-sp, (sc in next ch-sp, ch 3) 3 times, skip next ch-

sp, (3 dc, place stitch marker) in next pineapple shell; leave rem st un-worked.

Row 26. Ch 3; turn. 2 dc in first dc, skip next ch-sp, (sc in next ch-sp, ch 3) twice, skip next ch-sp, 3 dc in t-ch.

Row 27. Ch 3; turn. 2 dc in first dc, skip next ch-sp, sc in next ch-sp, ch 3, skip next ch-sp, 3 dc in t-ch.

Row 28. Ch 2; turn. 2 dc in first dc, skip 2 ch-sp, 3 dc in t-ch.

Row 29. Ch 3; turn. Skip 5 dc, sl st in t-ch.

Row 30. Turn. (3 sc, picot, 2 sc, sl st) in ch-sp. Finish off.

Finish Remaining Pineapples
With RS facing, join yarn with sl st in last marked pineapple shell of Row 25.

Row 25. Ch 3, 2 dc in same pineapple shell as joining, skip next ch-sp, (sc in next ch-sp, ch 3) 3 times, skip next ch-sp, (3 dc, place stitch marker) in next pineapple shell; leave rem st un-worked.

Rows 26-30. Work as for Rows 26-30 above.

Finish off.

Repeat finishing instructions for each remaining pineapple.

Top Edge
Close the gap at the top edge of the Skirt as follows:

1. Thread the 6-inch tail that was left at the beginning through a yarn needle. Fold the Skirt in half and insert the yarn needle into the first stitch of Row 1.

2. Pull the tail through the stitch to close the gap. Wrap the tail around the stitch 2 more times to secure, then knot it and weave in remaining tail. Continue with Top Edge.

With RS facing, join yarn with sl st in top edge of Skirt.

Rnd 1. Ch 1; sc evenly around top of Skirt, working an even number of sc. Join with sl st in first sc in rnd.

Rnd 2. Ch 4; turn. Skip first 2 sc, *dc in next sc, ch 1, skip next sc; rep from * around. Join with sl st in 3rd ch of t-ch.

Rnd 3. Ch 1; turn. *Sc in next ch-sp, sc in next sc; rep from * around. Join with sl st in first sc in rnd. Finish off.

Skirt Tie
Ch 148 (**148**, 166, **184**, 202, **220**, 220, **220**, 238). Finish off. Knot both ends and trim excess tail.

Bird of Paradise Bust Shaping Diagram

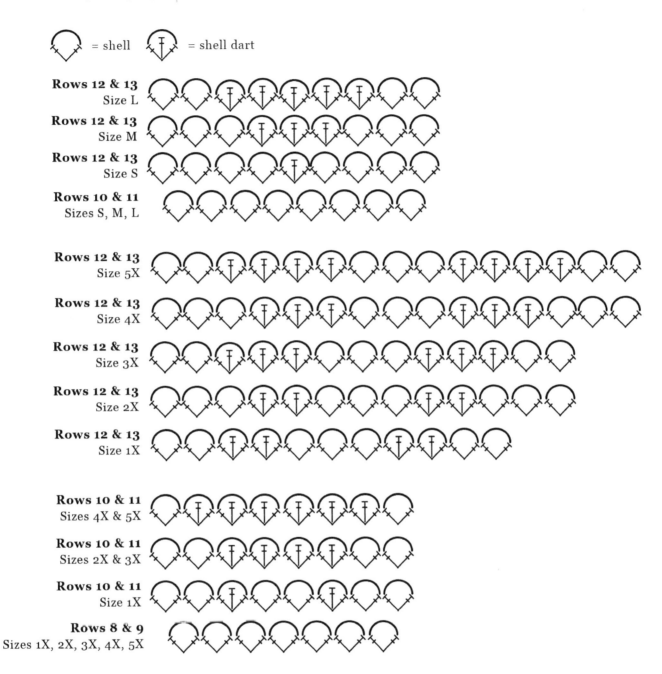

Bohemian Opulence Scarf

This design was inspired by vintage photos of belly dancers from the 1920s who created an exotic, indulgent look from wardrobe pieces already popular amongst the flappers. The motifs are worked in join-as-you-go fashion so that there is no assembly needed at the end.

Pattern Level

Complex / Complexe / Complejo

Finished Size

Women's XS (**S/M**, L/1X, **2X/3X**, 4X/5X)

Materials

- MC: 3 (**5**, 7, **9**, 11) oz 3/sport-weight yarn
- CC: 3 (**5**, 7, **9**, 11) oz 3/sport-weight yarn
- Size H-8 (6.0mm) crochet hook or size to obtain gauge
- Yarn needle

Gauge

1 triangular motif = 7 inches wide (blocked)

Special Stitches

2-dtr cluster. *YO 3 times and insert hook in indicated stitch, YO and pull yarn through the stitch, YO and pull yarn through 2 loops on the hook, 3 times; rep from * once more. YO and pull through all loops on the hook.

3-dtr cluster. *YO 3 times and insert hook in indicated stitch, YO and pull yarn through the stitch, YO and pull yarn through 2 loops on the hook, 3 times; rep from * twice more. YO and pull through all loops on the hook.

First Motif

Flower

With MC, ch 6. Join with sl st in first ch to form a ring.

Rnd 1. Ch 1; 9 sc in ring. Join with sl st in first sc. *9 sc.*

Rnd 2. Ch 1, *sc in next sc, ch 3; rep from * around. Join with sl st in first sc. *9 ch-sp.*

Rnd 3. (Sc, ch 9, sc) in ea ch-sp around. Join with sl st in first sc. *9 ch-sp.*

Rnd 4. (2 sc, 2 hdc, 3 dc, tr, 3dc, 2 hdc, 2 sc) in ea ch-sp around. Join with sl st in first sc. Finish off. *9 petals.*

Background

Join CC with sl st in tr of any petal.

Rnd 5. (Ch 6, sl st in tr of next petal) 8 times, ch 3, dc in tr of first petal. *9 ch-sp.*

Rnd 6. *Ch 6, sc in next ch-sp, ch 6, work corner: (3-dtr cluster, [ch 5, 2-dtr cluster in top of last cluster] twice, 3-dtr) in next ch-sp; corner made. Ch 6, sc in next ch-sp; rep from * twice more. Ch 6, join with sl st in dc. Finish off. *3 corners and 6 ch-sp.*

Subsequent Motifs

Rnds 1-5 of each subsequent are worked exactly the same as the First Motif.

Rnd 6 is also worked the same as the First Motif, except that it will be joined to the previous motifs at the corners as shown in the diagram.

Corner Joining

When you are ready to start a corner join, modify the corner instructions of Rnd 6 as follows: 3-dtr cluster in next ch-sp of current motif, ch 5, 2-dtr cluster in top of last cluster of current motif, sl st between the two 2-dtr clusters of the corner of the previous motif being joined to, ch 5, 2-dtr cluster in same space as sl st, 3-dtr cluster in same ch-sp as last 3-dtr cluster in current motif; corner join complete. Continue the rest of Rnd 6 as directed in First Motif.

Border

Join CC with sl st in any corner.

Rnd 1. Ch 1, *6 sc in side of next cluster, **6 sc in ea of next 3 ch-sp, 6 sc in side of ea of next 2 clusters; rep from ** across to corner motif, 6 sc in ea of next 3 ch-sp, 6 sc in side of next cluster, 3 sc in corner; rep from * around. Join with sl st in first sc in rnd. *369 (459, 549, 639, 729) sc.*

Border is worked in rows from this point forward.

Row 1. Ch 1, sc in same sc as joining, *ch 9, skip next 5 sc, sc in next sc, rep from * across to corner, ch 9, skip 1 sc, sc in next sc, **ch 9, skip next 5 sc, sc in next sc, rep from ** across to corner. Leave third edge unworked. *41 (51, 61, 71, 81) ch-sp.*

Row 2. Ch 1; turn. (3 sc, picot, 5 sc, picot, 3 sc) in ea ch-sp across.

Row 3. Ch 11; turn. Skip next 5 sc, *sc in next sc, ch 9, skip next 10 sc; rep from * across to corner. (Sc, ch 9, sc) in 5th sc of corner, **ch 9, skip next 10

sc, sc in next sc; rep from ** across to corner, ending last rep with ch 6, dtr in last sc.

Row 4. Ch 1; turn. (3 sc, picot, 3 sc) in first ch-sp, (3 sc, picot, 5 sc, picot, 3 sc) in ea rem ch-sp around to last ch-sp, (3 sc, picot, 3 sc) in last ch-sp.

Row 5. Ch 1; turn. *Sc in next sc, ch 9, skip next 10 sc; rep from * across to corner. (Sc, ch 9, sc) in 5th sc of corner, **ch 9, skip next 10 sc, sc in next sc; rep from ** across to corner.

Row 6. Rep Row 2. Finish off.

Block for best results.

Bohemian Opulence Assembly Diagram

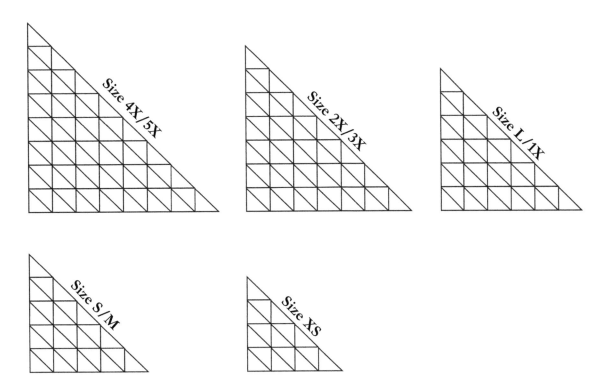

Size Charts

Women

Dimension	XS	S	M	L	1X	2X	3X	4X	5X
Bicep	10"	10"	11"	12"	13.5"	15.5"	17"	18.5"	19.5"
Wrist	5.75"	6.25"	6.5"	7"	7.5"	7.5"	8.5"	9.5"	10.5"
Cross back (shoulder to shoulder)	14.5"	15"	16.5"	17.5"	17.5"	18"	18"	18.5"	19"
Bust	30"	34"	38"	42"	46"	50"	54"	58"	62"
Bra cup	A	A	B	C	D	DD	DDD	DDD	DDD
Under bust	26"	29"	32"	35"	38"	41"	44"	48"	52"
Waist	24"	26.5"	30"	34"	38"	42"	45"	47"	50"
Hips	34"	36"	40"	44"	48"	53"	55"	57"	62"

Girls

Dimension	2T	4T	6	8	10	12	14	16
Bicep	7"	7.5"	8"	8.5"	8.75"	9"	9.25"	9.5"
Cross back (shoulder to shoulder)	9.25"	9.75"	10.25"	10.75"	11.25"	12"	12.25"	13"
Hips	22"	23.5"	25"	28"	29.5"	31.5"	33"	35.5"

Leg Warmers

Dimension	2–5 years	5–9 years	7–13 years	Adult Small	Adult Medium	Adult Large
Calf	9"	9.75"	10.5"	10.5"	12"	13.5"

Abbreviations and Stitch Glossary

Abbreviation	Term	Instructions
beg	beginning	
blo	back loops only	Crochet the stitch as usual, using only the back loop of the stitch being worked into.
ch-sp	chain space	
ch	chain	Yarn over and pull a loop through the loop on the hook.
dc	double crochet	1. YO and insert hook in indicated stitch. 2. YO and pull yarn through the stitch. 3. YO and pull yarn through 2 loops on the hook, twice.
dtr	double treble crochet	1. YO 3 times and insert hook in indicated stitch. 2. YO and pull yarn through the stitch. 3. YO and pull yarn through 2 loops on the hook, 4 times.
ea	each	
flo	front loops only	Crochet the stitch as usual, using only the front loop of the stitch being worked into.
hdc	half-double crochet	1. YO and insert hook in indicated stitch. 2. YO and pull yarn through the stitch. 3. YO and pull yarn through all 3 loops on the hook.
mm	millimeter	
picot	picot	Ch 3, sl st in last stitch.
rem	remaining	
rep	repeat	
rnd	round	
RS	right side	
sc	single crochet	1. Insert hook in indicated stitch. 2. YO and pull yarn through the stitch. 3. YO and pull yarn through all 3 loops on the hook.
sl st	slip stitch	1. Insert hook in indicated stitch. 2. YO and pull yarn through the stitch and the loop on the hook.
sp	space	
st	stitch	
t-ch	turning chain	
tog	together	1. Work the indicated number of stitches, ending each stitch before the final pull-through.

Abbreviation	Term	Instructions
		2. YO and pull yarn through all remaining loops on hook.
tr	treble crochet	1. YO twice and insert hook in indicated stitch.
		2. YO and pull yarn through the stitch.
		3. YO and pull yarn through 2 loops on the hook, 3 times.
trtr	triple treble crochet	1. YO 4 times and insert hook in indicated stitch.
		2. YO and pull yarn through the stitch.
		3. YO and pull yarn through 2 loops on the hook, 3 times.
WS	wrong side	
YO	yarn over	Bring the yarn up behind the hook.

Lightning Source UK Ltd.
Milton Keynes UK
UKHW051855090223
416667UK00010B/378

9 781736 955147